# LIVING IN
# MOROCCO

عنزلة مه

دلالة دلالة

With over 340 colour photographs

Photographs by Lisl Dennis
Text by Landt Dennis

# LIVING IN
# MOROCCO

## Design from Casablanca
## to Marrakesh

Thames and Hudson

**PAGES 2—3:**
In spring, kasbahs and ksour—
such as these in the Dades Valley
on the edge of the
Sahara—are surrounded by
orchards in bloom.

**PAGES 4—5:**
Crenellated walls
wrap around Asilah,
a fishing village and artists'
colony on the Atlantic
coast near Tangier.

**PAGES 6—7:**
This detail of a 17th-century
illuminated manuscript
in Arabic is from the collection
of noted scholar
Mohamed Sijelmassi.

**PAGES 8—9:**
A palm stands in
stark contrast to the soft red
walls of Essaouira.

**PAGES 10—11:**
Whitewash covers the
walls of the tomb of a *marabout*,
or holy man, in Safi.

First Published in Great Britain in 1992 by Thames
and Hudson Ltd, London, by arrangement with
Clarkson N. Potter, Inc.,
201 East 50th Street, New York, NY 10022

Reprinted in 1998

British Library Cataloguing-in-Publication Data
A catalogue record for this book is available from the
British Library

ISBN 0-500-01545-7

Printed and bound in Japan

Tunisia is a woman, Algeria is a man, Morocco is a lion.
*Arab saying*

The first thing one should own is a home; and it is the last thing one should sell, for a home is one's tomb this side of heaven.
*Moroccan proverb*

When things come from the heart, the world is very small.
*Hassan II, King of Morocco*

# Contents

# Introduction

THE FILM *CASABLANCA* AND ITS CAST—INGRID BERGMAN, HUMPHREY BO-
gart, Claude Rains, and Sydney Greenstreet—are legendary. But what of
Morocco? ✋ A Muslim country with a population of 24 million—65 percent
are Arab, 35 percent Berber—Morocco is a constitutional monarchy roughly
the size of California. Morocco is separated from Europe by the Strait of
Gibraltar, bordered by the Atlantic Ocean to the west and the Mediterranean
to the north. Algeria is to the east; Mauritania and the Sahara Desert are to
the south. The Rif Mountains hug the Mediterranean coast; the Anti Atlas,
High Atlas, and Middle Atlas mountains form the country's spine. In fact,
70 percent of Morocco is mountainous. ✋ Morocco has an almost unequaled
climate. Days of sun and year-round temperatures ranging from the forties
to the nineties Fahrenheit allow for a wide range of flora and fauna—from
oaks, pines, and palms to cork, cedar, eucalyptus, and citrus trees. In the
spring, before the summer heat, wildflowers grow in profusion along the
coastal plains and in the valleys. Orange and yellow marigolds, white daisies
and narcissi, pink oleander and asphodels, blue mallows, gorse, and broom
blanket the countryside. Private gardens run riot with daffodils, tulips, vi-
olets, jasmine, irises, roses, hibiscus, and geraniums. ✋ The Moroccan landscape varies dramatically. In the west, along the Atlantic shoreline, it is flat
and agrarian, with acres of wheat and olive groves. In the north, on the

**A Berber motif
decorates the striking
narrow stairwell
of this contemporary
Marrakesh house.**

Mediterranean, the verdant Rif Mountains spill into the sea. Across the plain toward the south and down the middle of the country, the Anti, Middle, and High Atlas mountains loom up against a brilliant blue sky, their caps snow-covered in winter. Southern Morocco is mostly desert, but the harsh, wind-swept, endless expanses do contain oases of date palms, fruit orchards, and roses. ✋ The story of Morocco begins with the Berbers, who are believed to have migrated originally from the Caucasus. Fair-skinned, often blue-eyed, Berbers comprise a significant part of the population of Morocco. The Berbers arrived in Morocco around 1500 B.C. and developed major trade routes with the black kingdoms of West Africa. Some nomadic, others sedentary agriculturalists, the many hundreds of different patriarchal, polygamous Berber tribes—with their separate languages (only the Tuaregs of the Sahara have a written Berber language)—also traded with seafaring Phoenicians and Carthaginians who landed on the shores of what was then Mauritania. ✋ By the last century B.C. the Romans—who, incidentally, called the Berbers *Barbari*, hence "barbarian"—ruled Mauritania. Among the more noteworthy of Mauritania's governors was Juba II—noteworthy in the main for his marriage to Cleopatra Silene, daughter of Marc Antony and Cleopatra. In A.D. 683 there was a shift in power. An Arab army under the command of Oqba ben Nafi swept across Africa from the Near East.

Settling in Morocco, these new conquerors introduced Islam as the religion of the country, which they called *El Maqhreb al Aqsa*, "The Land of the Far West." At the same time began a succession of Moroccan dynasties, among them the Idrisids, Almoravids, Almohads, Merinids, Saadians, and the current Alawites. With a base firmly established in Morocco, the Arabs were anxious to continue their attempt to convert the world to Islam. In A.D. 711 Tariq ibn Ziyad and his army of twelve thousand sailed across the Strait of Gibraltar from Morocco's Jabal Musa, one of the Pillars of Hercules, and began their conquest of Spain. ✋ During the eight hundred years the Arab Moroccans, or Moors, remained in Spain, additional Arabs continued to move into Morocco from the Near East. In A.D. 788 Moulay Idris, a descendant of the Prophet, and his followers fled there after defeat in battle near Mecca. In Morocco, he was accepted as ruler and forcefully persuaded the Berbers to convert from agrarian animism to Islam. Today, Berbers practice both animism and Islam. While the Arabs prospered in Morocco, the Moors were under constant attack from Spanish Christians and began to lose their control of southern Spain. They were forced out of Valencia in 1094, Zaragoza in 1118, Córdoba in 1236, and Seville in 1248. Finally, by 1492, when Ferdinand and Isabella captured Granada, the Moors were in full retreat back to Morocco. ✋ Morocco's extraordinarily large number of skilled ar-

**Slender minarets
rise from the
roof scape of Fez.**

tisans trace their father-to-son craftsmanship to this mass exodus of ex-Andalusians who reestablished their businesses on the North African side of the Strait of Gibraltar. Settling mostly in the four Imperial Cities—Fez, Marrakesh, Rabat, and Meknes—in a country never conquered by the Ottomans and therefore uniquely free from Turkish influences, these artisans introduced a distinct Hispano-Moorish style, one that continues to be purer and stronger than any found in other Arab nations today. ✋ By the beginning of the 18th century and throughout the 19th, adventurous Europeans were drawn to the exotic enchantment of North Africa. Often forced to camp for weeks outside a Moroccan city's walls before getting a local ruler's permission to enter, they were frequently rewarded by lavish and extended hospitality. Glowing descriptions in the diaries of intrepid travelers tell of courts where thousands of veiled women of the harem, rifle-bearing tribesmen, and turbaned slaves stumbled over one another to make the newcomers happy. According to Walter Harris, the London *Times* correspondent in Morocco at the turn of the 19th century, "compliments flowed as fast as mountain streams, happy in their wording, sonorous in their utterances, and absolutely insincere." ✋ Even at the turn of this century Moroccans were engaged in fierce, long-standing intertribal warfare. Rich with sultanic intrigue, the country was medieval in many ways. The gates of Fez were closed

**Sunset turns the adobe walls of Marrakesh red.**

at sunset each night, the walls of the city decorated with the cut-off heads of criminals displayed on spikes. ✋ The Germans, the English, the French, and the Spanish all felt Morocco needed "protection," and each foreign nation sought to convince the sultan that it was the one to provide it. Finally Sultan Moulay Hafid agreed. Under attack and anxious for foreign aid, he signed the Treaty of Fez in 1912, giving the French the right to occupy southern Morocco and the Spanish the right to northern Morocco. ✋ The first resident-general (later marshall), Louis Lyautey, sought to pacify as well as to preserve the country during the French Protectorate. He was scrupulously careful not to undermine Islam or destroy any monuments and decreed that all new construction would be outside the ancient cities and kasbahs in the *Nouvelle Ville*, or New City. He was also instrumental in the building of the ports of Casablanca and Kenitra and saw to it that a modern educational system was introduced, government administration modernized, and the legal system reformed. Finally, during the Protectorate, peace was established among the feuding tribesmen. Cultivation of crops, vineyards, and cattle raising began. Roads and railroads were built. And phosphate, Morocco's major export, was discovered. ✋ By the 1950s and 1960s, Morocco's laissez-faire attitude toward foreign residents and their life-styles had become a magnet for many. Tangier in particular was haven for hedonist, writer,

**Snow caps the
High Atlas Mountains
even in summer.**

23

and artist alike. Barbara Hutton, Paul Bowles, Elias Canetti, Joe Orton, Jean Genet, and William Burroughs were among the countless hundreds who were captivated by the mystery and hypnotic foreboding that the city and the rest of Morocco exuded. They found, too, that the country's paradoxical combination of vivid sensuality and intense spirituality—which was evident in the canvases of such artists as Delacroix, Géricault, and Matisse, who painted in Morocco in the late 19th and early 20th centuries—still held strong. ✋ In 1956, during the reign of Mohammed V, Morocco gained independence from France and Spain. Today his son, Hassan II, is sovereign head of the Kingdom of Morocco. And despite increased tourism a good deal of the country remains miraculously and refreshingly removed from the rest of the world. ✋ Of special significance, traditional Moroccan architectural and artistic craftsmanship is flourishing. A major reason is that King Hassan personally promotes the nation's ancient tradition of crafts. Anxious to keep Moroccan workers in gypsum and tile and painters of wood employed, Hassan II commissioned a magnificent mausoleum for his father in the capital, Rabat. He initiated the renovation of numerous ancient mosques, universities, and royal palaces and is responsible for the construction of the Hassan II mosque in Casablanca, expected to be the country's finest example of contemporary Moroccan craftsmanship and perhaps one of the finest ex-

**A massive arch marks an entrance to the town of Essaouira.**

amples of Islamic design in the world. ♛ An estimated 2 million Moroccans, approximately 20 percent of the nation's working population, earn their livelihoods in craft production. Thousands more, both men and women, are in government-sponsored craft schools. Rugs, the fourth major export, account for roughly 45 percent of all crafts in Morocco. Another 20 percent are leathercrafts and 17 percent are ceramics and pottery. ♛ The mournful wail of a half dozen muezzins calling the faithful to prayer in Fez; the hoot of an owl, the song of a nightingale wafting through the orange-and-jasmine-perfumed air at the Hotel Gazelle d'Or in Taroudant; the red glow of sunset on the snow-covered High Atlas Mountains beyond the crenellated walls surrounding the garden at the Hotel La Mamounia in Marrakesh—to travel in Morocco is a sensual, stimulating, tantalizing experience. ♛ So much to see. So much to buy. Handwoven baskets, olive jars, embroidery, hand-painted boxes, Berber jewelry, amulets, camel saddles, and rugs. The owners of the houses photographed for this book have had a great opportunity to search the souk when decorating their properties. They live in one of the world's most artistic nations. As guests in their homes, readers of this book are able to appreciate the skill and imagination these Moroccan and foreign homeowners have shown in using the nation's decorative arts and crafts in their houses' architecture and in furnishings.

**Berber women cross the Sahara with fodder.**

# Three Habitats

THREE TRADITIONAL WAYS IN WHICH PEOPLE CREATED PLACES TO live in Morocco bear witness to a remarkably varied geography. They testify as well to differing life-styles. ♥ City palaces conform to the Arab tradition of maintaining privacy. Exterior details were minimized lest they reveal the owner's wealth. Interiors, however, with striking tiled courtyards, were lavishly "furnished" with fabulous Moroccan craftsmanship. ♥ In the country stand ancient crenellated Berber kasbahs. Berbers pay special attention to the exterior decoration of their barely furnished dwellings and adorn their kasbahs' adobe exteriors with whitewashed motifs. ♥ In the Atlas and along the salt marshes bordering the Atlantic, Berber nomads pitch their tents. Multistriped and woven of animal hair, the tents are indistinguishable from the scorched earth of summer.

**Perforations—outlined in white in the adobe wall and tower of a Berber kasbah in the southern Sahara— provide needed ventilation to kasbah interiors.**

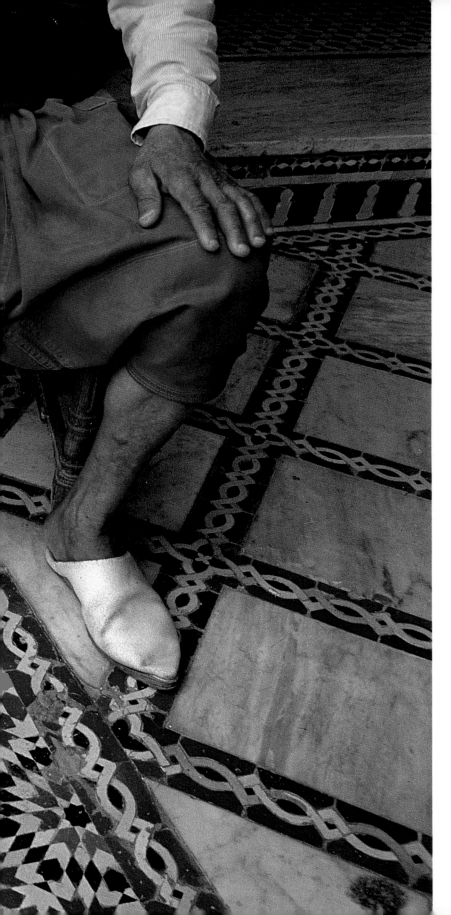

# Palaces

VERY LARGE AND VERY SPLEN-
didly decorated—truly grand private houses more than anything—
Moroccan palaces were built and
lived in by monarchs and high
government officials as well as
wealthy merchants throughout
the country. It was in Fez, however, from the 16th through the
19th century, where Islamic palace architecture reached a pinna-
cle. The city's phenomenal wealth
and a local population of skilled
craftsmen led to the building of
some of the most elaborate and
luxurious palaces in the world.

As with all traditional building
in Morocco, absolute Islamic rules
of design prevailed. The "style"
of each palace was inevitably the
same: Hispano-Moorish. Differ-
ences lay in the number of rooms
and their degree of opulence.

**Fez is the location of the
Palais Mokri, built in
1910 for Tayeb Mokri.
The palace tiles come
from nearby kilns.**

31

OPPOSITE: *zwaq*, or painting on wood, is common throughout Morocco. ABOVE: wrought-iron stairs and balustrades were imported from Italy. RIGHT: caid Tayeb Mokri once stood at the top of the grand staircase to welcome guests.

Still, there was some European influence. In the late 16th century, for example, Moroccan palace builders traded sugar for Italian marble that was carved into columns. And by the late 19th and early 20th centuries, a few palaces, including the Palais Mokri (built in 1910 by Tayeb Mokri), incorporated stained-glass windows, crystal chandeliers, even wrought-iron staircase balustrades shipped in from Europe.

As with European castles, many Moroccan palaces were too large and too expensive to maintain and ultimately were abandoned. Fortunately, some are being restored, including the 18th-century Palais Tazi in Fez, owned by the Benjelloun family.

The 19th-century Bahia palace in Marrakesh (built by Ba Ahmed, Vizier of Hassan I) has already been brought back to life.

**A German Rud-Ibach-Sohn piano with a rare half-circular keyboard sits covered with years of dust in the music room of the Palais Mokri.**

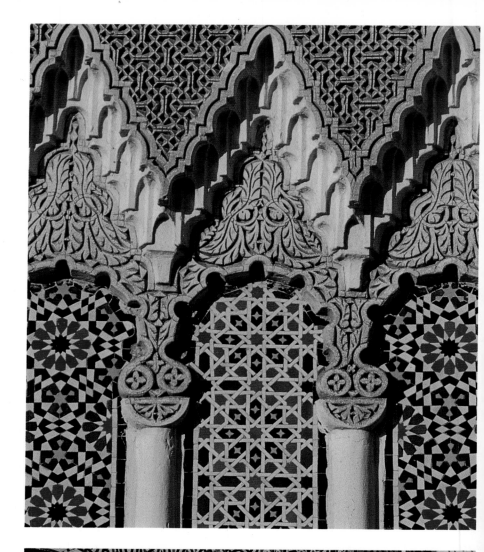

Its benefactor is King Hassan II, who moves frequently from one royal palace to another throughout the Imperial Cities of Rabat, Fez, Marrakesh, and Meknes.

Surrounded by massive gates and high walls, the royal palaces are huge; the royal palace in Fez, for instance, covers one hundred acres. In addition to *zelliges*, or tiles, they incorporate several "royal palace features," including *germuds*, or green tile roofs, and *jamurs*—roof spikes incorporating from one to five glistening brass balls of increasing size. *Jamurs* are frequently surmounted by the national emblem, the Moroccan star inside a crescent.

Palace building continues in Morocco. Under construction for more than ten years, His Majesty's residence in Agadir is reputed to contain the finest examples of modern-day Islamic design and craftsmanship in the kingdom, perhaps even in the world.

**TOP: decorating a room, courtyard, or entrance with a succession of tile friezes of varying widths, patterns, and colors is common throughout Morocco. BOTTOM: modern tiles laid in age-old designs, traditional plasterwork, and calligraphy surround the doors of the royal palace in Fez.**

The king's many palaces display the finest Moroccan craftsmanship, as seen in these enormous contemporary brass doors in Fez.

**BOTH PAGES:** the Bahia palace in Marrakesh is an example of 19th-century Andalusian-style domestic architecture. Of unusual significance is its undecorated, multicolored wooden ceiling, OPPOSITE, a rare example of beauty unadorned.

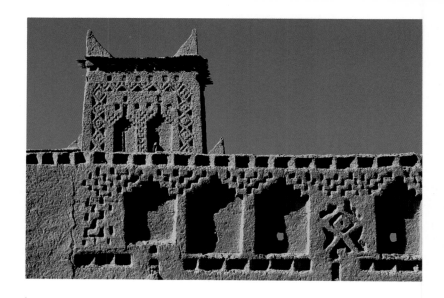

# Kasbahs and Ksour

BERBER STRONGHOLDS DATING from the 14th century, Moroccan kasbahs, monumental single-family fortresses, and ksour, fortified tribal villages, are dramatically located on plateaus towering over fertile valleys planted with fruit trees and grain. Kasbahs are especially conspicuous along the Dras, Dades, Todrha, and Tafilat river valleys on the eastern slopes of the Atlas Mountains; on the edges of date palm oases bordering the Sahara; and along what is commonly called the Route of the Kasbahs between the desert towns of Er-Rachidia and Quarzazate.

Built of *pisé,* or pounded red earth reinforced with straw, kasbahs with their enormous wooden gates and walled ksour appear like

**BOTH PAGES:** only occasionally visited by its owners, who live in Casablanca, this adobe kasbah in the highly decorated village of Amerhidl in the southern Sahara is slowly beginning to crumble.

BELOW: kasbahs and ksour grow in size as families expand, leading to infinite doors and courtyards.

OPPOSITE: both decorative and utilitarian, the incised openings in the kasbahs' walls are usually outlined in cream-colored paint and provide much needed ventilation in the intense summer heat. ABOVE: some of Morocco's most handsome ksour cling to the sides of the Dades Valley in the southern Sahara, surrounded by hundreds of acres of date palms and fruit trees.

gigantic mirages against brilliant blue horizons. Unlike discreet Arab town houses of the north, with their plain exteriors and hidden luxurious interiors built around courtyards, kasbahs willingly show their faces to the world, with adobe exteriors that are often embellished with bold, geometric Berber motifs incised or painted in white. Inside, however, kasbahs and ksour are honeycombs of dark, narrow passageways leading to lookout points, grain rooms, and animal shelters. Here there are no fine painted ceilings or tiles.

Once stopover points for camel caravans going through the great Tizi n'Tishka and Tizi n'Test passes of the High Atlas Mountains en route to Timbuktu to trade for gold, amber, ostrich feathers, and animal skins, many kasbahs and ksour are empty today. They are windswept, sandblasted, and fast turning to ruins.

**This 19th-century ksar, Ait Benhaddou, is near Quarzazate in the southern Sahara. It has appeared as a location in several epic films, including *Lawrence of Arabia*.**

# Tents

BERBER SHEPHERDS LIVE IN TENTS when they take their sheep to pasture in the Atlas Mountains or along the salt marshes on the Atlantic and Mediterranean coastlines. Upon arrival at a campsite, the men drive the first peg, or *adriq*, into the ground. The women then set up the tent, dividing it in two; one side for themselves, the other for the men and important visitors. Finally, herbs are scattered on the ground inside the tent to ensure protection and prosperity.

Moroccan *flij*, or tent strips, are usually sixty centimeters wide and are clamped or sewn together. Handwoven from sheep wool and goat hair, tent material is predominantly black and brown, with shadings of beige, tan, and off-white. From a distance, and in

**LEFT: each spring, thousands of tribesmen pitch *makhzens*, or festival tents, outside the royal palace in Marrakesh to honor the king on Throne Day. OPPOSITE: traditional Berber tents are made of strips handwoven from sheep wool and goat hair.**

ABOVE: *makhzens* are lined with *ha'iti*, or wall coverings, made of strips of appliquéd fabric that are pieced together.
LEFT: upon arrival at a campsite, Berber men drive the first peg, or *adriq*, into the ground.

149·6 l 3

summer especially, Moroccan tents often blend in with the parched, rugged landscape, becoming totally camouflaged. Inside, dozens of rugs are laid out on the floor and stacked in piles six to ten feet high. Large, textured pillows are strewn about for sitting and sleeping.

*Makhzens*, or festival tents, are traditionally put up in the countryside by chiefs for their personal use during important tribal gatherings and other special events. Made from heavy white canvas, these *caidal* tents are usually decorated outside with black leather depicting crenellation and *qandils*, or oil lamps.

On Throne Day each spring, dozens of *makhzens* are set up in the campground outside the Marrakesh palace of His Majesty King Hassan II. Members of the court, visitors, and foreign dignitaries are entertained at lavish banquets

**TOP: rugs are hung from the sides on Berber tents as insulation. CENTER: wrapped tightly in swaddling bands, a Berber baby sleeps on a handwoven blanket. BOTTOM: wool embroidery often decorates Berber tents.**

inside the tents. Outside, tribesmen stage *fantasias* throughout the day. As many as two dozen tribesmen will gallop across the field in a straight line, pull their horses to an abrupt stop, raise their rifles into the air, and fire in dramatic unison.

Today people living in Moroccan cities often buy Berber shepherd and caidal tents to put in their gardens for parties.

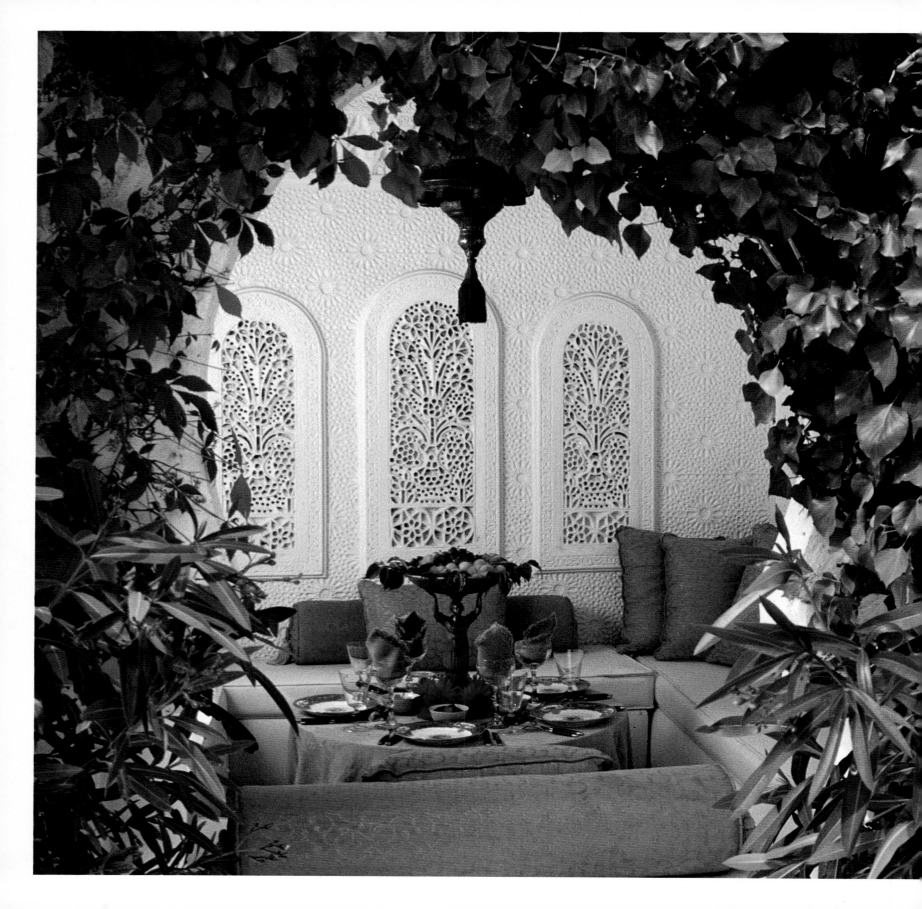

# Life
# Outdoors

WARM DAYS, COOL EVENINGS, THE SCENT OF NIGHT-FLOWERING
jasmine, a full moon over the snow-capped Atlas Mountains, whitewashed terraces overlooking the Mediterranean, courtyards with
splashing fountains and shimmering lanterns, the haunting melodies
of desert musicians and singers from Tafroute: the pleasures of outdoor living in Morocco have special appeal. ✋ Indeed, the traditional
Moroccan house is designed to combine indoor living with outdoor
living. With a *wust ed dar*, or courtyard, the house centers around a
*riyad*, or garden, whose raised pathways are made of tile or marble
and follow strict geometrical patterns dictated by Islam. ✋ In the
middle of the courtyard is a tile fountain, almost always strewn with
rose petals. Walls and pergolas are festooned with purple, apricot, and
white bougainvillea. Potted plants; roses; shasta daisies; delphiniums;

**In a white plaster of Paris rooftop pavillion in Tangier, cool green cotton cushions surround a Moroccan-style table.**

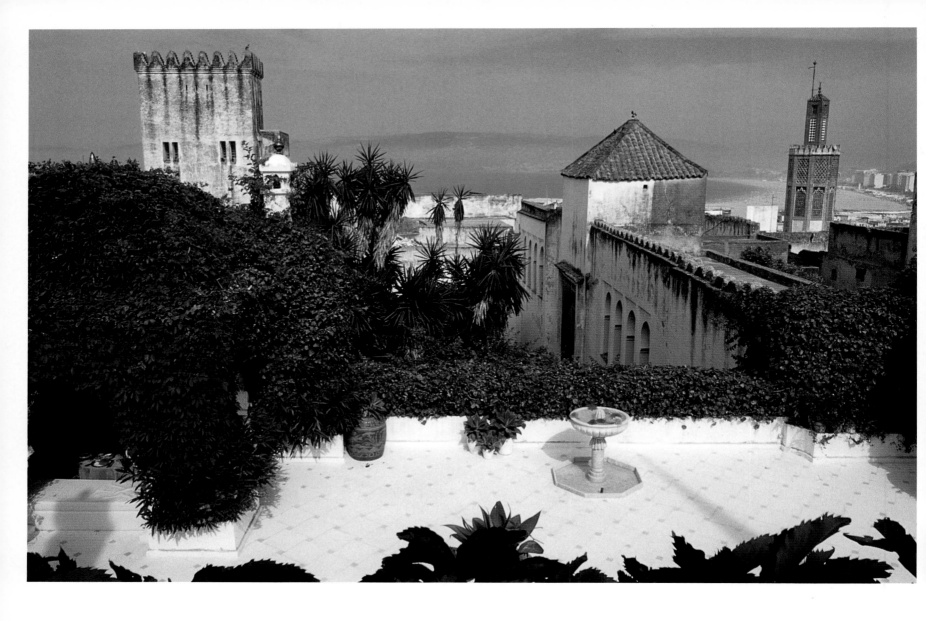

nasturtiums; geraniums; banana, lemon, and orange trees; cypresses; and palms—even stands of bamboo—add further to the house's lush, North African botanical environment.

In more recent years, European homeowners have introduced to Morocco the notion of rooftop terrace living. To sit out on or to entertain on one's rooftop terrace in the medina, "that is something a traditional Moroccan wouldn't do; the neighbors might see him,"

The rooftop
of an adobe-and-stone
house in the Ourika Valley
is set for lunch.
The Berber rugs are made of
straw and embroidery.

explains Adolpho de Velasco, a Spanish antiques dealer. De Velasco himself frequently invites friends to a candlelight dinner on his rug-covered terrace overlooking Tangier. "Terrace outdoor living is beginning to be appreciated, but it is definitely a new way of thinking in a country where privacy is a deeply rooted way of life," he says.

Pools and pool houses, lawns and European-style gardens—other than at hotels—are also only recently beginning to be appreciated by homeowners. The delay arises from two considerations. First, Islam calls for the body to be covered, not displayed in a bathing suit. Second, to use precious water in any way other than for necessities goes against drought-conscious Islamic tradition. Deeper wells and contemporary viewpoints have caused a change, however.

An Italo-Moorish loggia beside a courtyard swimming pool is for private entertaining. As is common in Morocco, heavy canvas curtains are pulled closed to keep the sun out. Murals of a romanticized Sahara are by Canadian artist Christopher Wangley; antique Berber pots bought in the local souk flank the pool.

Swimming pools
have only recently become
popular throughout
Morocco. This one—outside
a large modern house of
*pise*, or rammed earth, in
Marrakesh—does double
duty as a reflecting pool.

58

# Chaouen

PERCHED ON THE SIDE OF A DEEP RAVINE IN THE REMOTE, RUGGED Rif Mountains in northern Morocco, the village of Chaouen (Chechaouen) was founded in 1480 by Arab prince Ali ibn Rachid. Here, Muslims and Jews, fleeing Spain and Christian persecution, held out against repeated attacks. Chaouen also became a pilgrimage destination for Berber followers of Moulay Abdessalam ben Mchich. Patron saint of the local Djhebali tribesmen, he is buried in the nearby countryside. ✋ Off-limits to non-Muslims for centuries and only finally conquered by the Spanish in 1926 at the time of the Protectorate, Chaouen today welcomes visitors. They are immediately struck by the town's roofs, which are tiled and eaved, in contrast to the flat roofs found throughout the rest of Morocco, and speak of Chaouen's Andalusian heritage. Unspoiled because of years of isolation,

Chaouen has a shimmering "lunar" atmosphere. As if one continuous surface molded from plastic, stone walls, alcoves, Moorish arches, interior courtyards, and narrow cobbled streets are covered with whitewash that has been tinted a luminous, bone-chilling blue. Some say the color frightens mosquitoes away, others that it reduces the glare of the brilliant, high-altitude sunlight.

Here Spanish is heard more often than French and city life seems of another time. Black-eyed, olive-skinned housewives make furtive excursions, scurrying through aquamarine-colored, grottolike alleys to the fruit and vegetable market and the local bakery. Children kick balls and skip rope in front of studded bright blue doors. And old women lead donkeys in from the countryside with a nighttime supply of firewood from the nearby forests.

**Moroccan exterior doors-within-doors allow homeowners both privacy and protection. They are opened only as long as needed—for a visitor, a pack mule, a large delivery.**

A study in color and texture.
Exteriors of houses are
painted a bone-chilling
blue. Doors are often
studded in star patterns.
Courtyards are swept clean
with brushes. Pom-poms
decorate traditional
hats worn by Rif mountain
women, who bring
fodder into town each evening.

RIGHT: open-back *babouches,* or heelless slippers, are taken off before entering a Moroccan house. Men prefer plain colors— yellow for everyday, white to go to the mosque. Women's *babouches* are many colored and gaily embroidered. OPPOSITE: striped wool fabrics are often hung to air outside doorways.

TOP: Moroccan housewives take homemade bread dough to the nearest communal oven for baking. ABOVE: lace hangs in the deep window of a Chaouen house. OPPOSITE: Berber women pass the decorated entrance to a mosque.

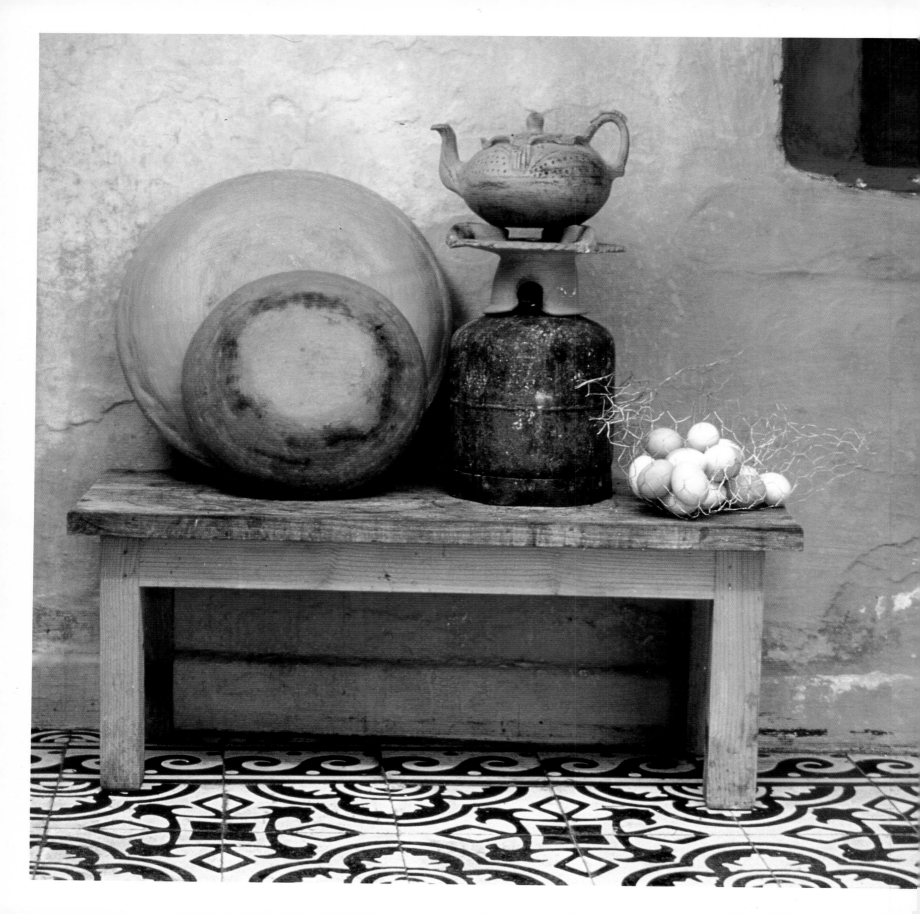

# A Rif Mountain Retreat

CHAOUEN DOESN'T READILY ACCEPT STRANGERS. IT TOOK JEAN LOU Guerin several years to convince his Berber landlord to rent him a 150-year-old, three-story property tucked away in an alley. Once there, he made it his own. ✋ "For me, the things of the spirit, not the things of a house, are what count," he confides. "That's why there's so little in my house." ✋ Indeed, a few decorative pots, hand-woven bedspreads, tables, and chairs comprise the house's "furnishings." Flour sacks stretched out on strings serve as sun shields. ✋ "Unlike locals in Chaouen, whose houses are primarily whitewashed inside, I added colors to the lye," Guerin says, motioning to the vibrant greens, rusts, pinks, and blues of walls, columns, and stairs. On the outside, he conforms to tradition and repaints several times a year with Chaouen's signature iceberg blue.

ABOVE: a steep flight of stairs with black-and-white Spanish tiles and melon-colored walls leads to the second floor. OPPOSITE: a storage and laundry room. The mottled effect is produced by the house's damp walls.

OPPOSITE: Guerin's strong artistic color sense is evident throughout the 150-year-old house. Each room is a different color. ABOVE: the house is built around a traditional Moroccan *riyad*, or courtyard, paved with brilliant tile. LEFT: prototypes for Guerin's colorful leatherwork. Made in his workshop, they are exported worldwide.

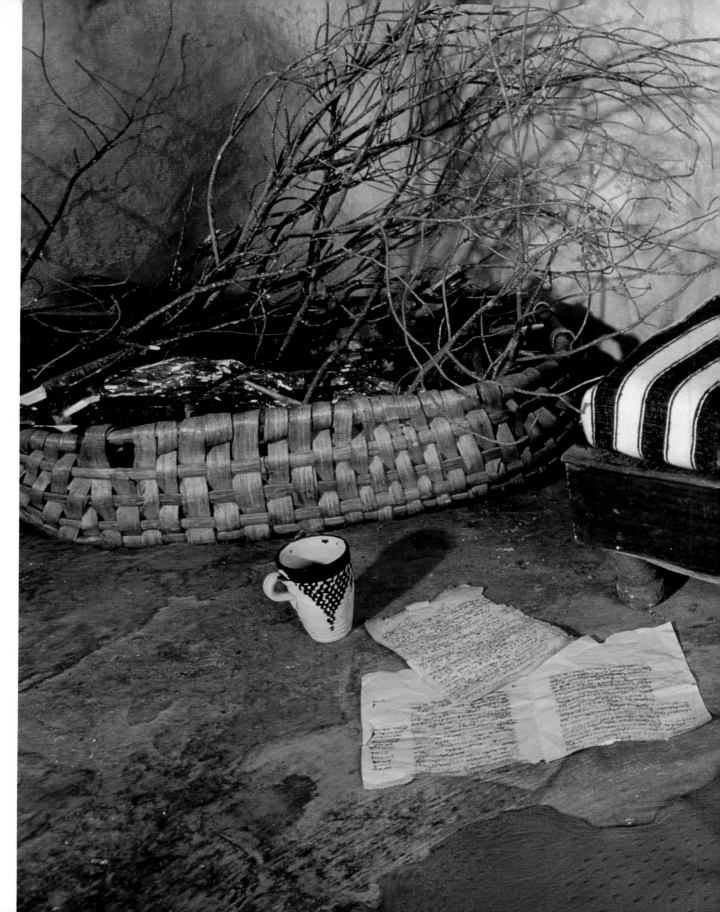

RIGHT: handwoven, black-and-white Berber material covers a cot. A goat-hide floor covering and a basketful of kindling complete the guest room furnishings. OPPOSITE, FROM TOP: a wood-burning stove heats the house in winter; the stool is made of cork. Guerin's courtyard workbench is covered with leathercraft tools. In a bedroom, a Berber carpet hangs over the bed and a Berber straw-and-wool rug covers the floor.

# A Touch of Spain

An old wooden chair is painted a striking flamenco red. Black-and-white floor tiles are from Spain. The red-and-white handwoven, wool material is a *courzya*, or apron, worn by local Berber women.

LONDON ART DEALER MICHAEL PARKINS, HIS WIFE, AND CHILDREN vacation in an eighty-year-old house in Chaouen. Inaccessible by car but only minutes by foot from Place Mohammed V with its crafts vendors and fruit and vegetable stalls, the *dar*, or house, is a classic example of Hispano–Moorish design whose Andalusian roots date to the 14th century. ✋ With its windowless outside walls built straight up from the street like a rampart, the Parkinses' hideaway typifies the age-old Moroccan homeowner's belief that conspicuous exteriors are a poor show. ✋ As in other Arab countries, a traditional Moroccan home is more than a place to live. It is a private enclosure for contemplation, an oasis away from the outside world. For centuries, isolation and intimacy have remained important to Moroccan homeowners. What is inside is nobody's business except the owner's.

RIGHT: A steep inside staircase leads down from the rooms surrounding a courtyard. OPPOSITE: like many foreigners, the Parkinses use Rif Mountains materials for decorating their house.

On the ground floor, the Parkinses' long, narrow, arcaded reception rooms open onto tiled *wust ed dar*, which allows maximum indoor-outdoor living. A staircase leads to upstairs bedrooms and additional living rooms that face the corridors overlooking the courtyard.

RIGHT: the souk in Quezzane near Chaouen is full of shops selling brightly colored, handpainted chests like this one. OPPOSITE: the Parkinses' second-floor bedrooms face onto a *riyad;* interior doors and windows admit air and light.

Strong primary colors are the principal decoration of the sparsely furnished house. The handwoven striped wool spread was bought in the souk.

82

ABOVE: the antique chest
and shelf are from Tétouan.
RIGHT: two Berber-style
plaster arches flank an Islamic
arch, separating a
ground-floor courtyard from
the main reception room. A
*haiti*, cut-out material
sewn together to decorate
the inside of a tent, is hung
on the wall. Local
handwoven material covers
two couches and
the banquettes. A bouquet of
fresh mint sits on a table.

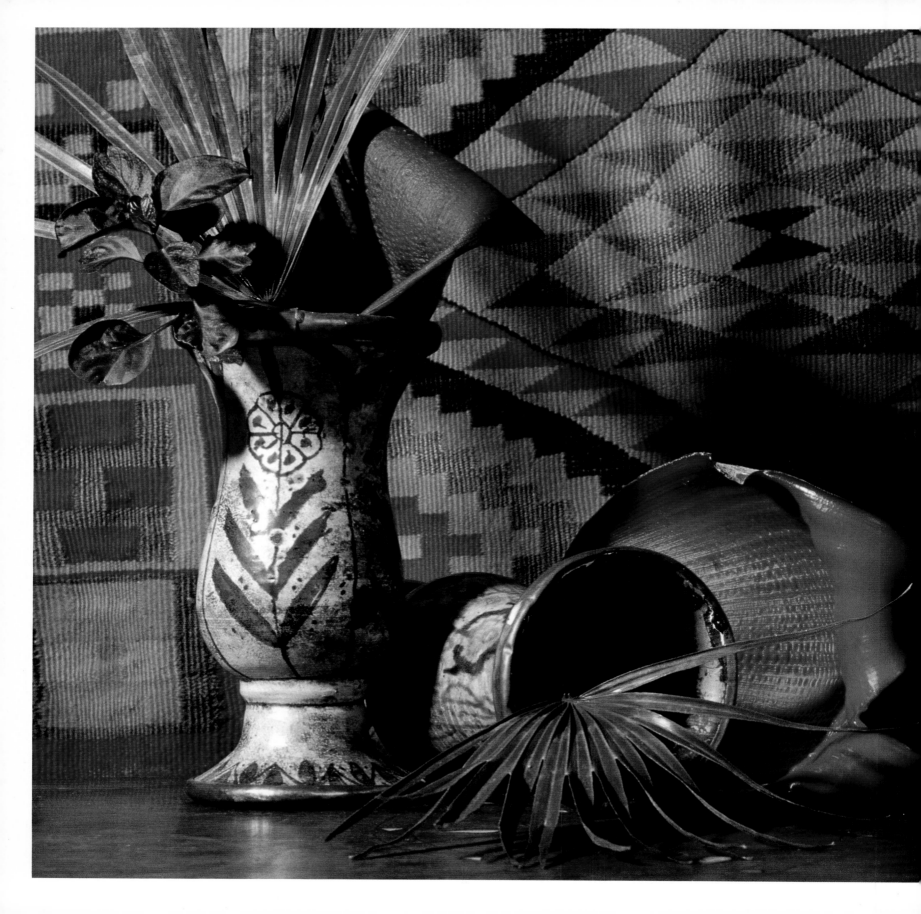

Textiles
Rugs
Leather
Pottery
Thuya Wood

# Folk Arts

**Homeowners in Morocco frequently decorate with antique rugs from North Africa and the Near East, which they turn into wall art.**

LIKE THE BERBERS, EARLY ARABS LIVED IN TENTS WITH FURNISHINGS that were utilitarian and able to be strapped to a horse or camel. They may not have been luxury items, but tremendous skill went into their making. ✋ Inspired by their king, Moroccans have a renewed appreciation of their Berber and Islamic traditions. King Hassan has triggered a renaissance in the country's arts and crafts, many of which trace their Hispano-Moorish origins to the Moors' flight from Spain in the 15th century. ✋ Blessed with ample artisans who·can produce custom-made furniture and accessories at a fraction of what it would cost in Europe or the United States, Moroccans frequently commission all the furnishings for their houses. Although many modern-day Moroccans have European furniture in their houses, it is almost always combined with their own country's arts and crafts.

# Textiles

FOR CENTURIES, MOROCCANS and Berbers have produced a rich variety of textiles, many of which are embroidered. Different styles of historic Moroccan and Berber textiles are easily recognized by collectors. Rabat workmanship is solid and robust. Fez is known for its delicate, aesthetic sense. Meknes textiles are heavy and primitive. Curious symbols representing exotic birds, dragons, and chimera are found in textiles from the seaport of Salé and from the trade route centers of Tétouan and Azemmour—evidence of exposure to patterns from Europe and central Africa.

Although local mills, particularly in Fez, now mass-produce textiles in both traditional and contemporary designs, most Moroccans continue to dress in hand-woven—and handmade—cloth-

**Women in Essaouira dress in all-white, -black, or -brown *haiks*, or robes, and wear veils. When visiting outside, they face a wall to avoid eye contact with men and strangers.**

ing. Women are particularly proud of their caftans, which are made throughout the country in thousands of all-male caftan workshops. Men wear *djellabas*, or robes. In winter, they also wear *burnooses*, or woolen cloaks.

Embroidery on sophisticated silk brocades and on the more prosaic linens and wools was the work of young women, usually for their trousseaus. Unlike European and American samplers, this work was never signed. But the woman could express individuality through her interpretation of the traditional motifs: stars, rosettes, the hand of Fatima, tulips, narcissus, cypress trees, scorpions, centipedes—even lice. They could also personalize their handiwork by their choice of colors. Silk threads of mauve, blue, gray, brown, and black make up the Moroccan palette; Berber

OPPOSITE: a traditional palace uniform on a soldier guarding the mausoleum of Mohammed V in Rabat. RIGHT: multipatterned and richly woven with metallic threads, antique and contemporary textiles are often combined with brightly colored embroidery.

ABOVE: silk-embroidered
wedding belts from Fez
are prized by collectors.
RIGHT: women dancers
wear dresses from
the Sahara at the annual
Festival of the Rose
in El-Kelaa-des-Mgouna.

Machine-made textiles
are often used as coverings for
pillows sold in the souk.

91

Moroccan textiles used for clothing and for interior design range in color from subtle to vibrant, in design from naive to sophisticated. Here is part of Morocco's bounty: rugs airing high in the Atlas Mountains, contemporary pillows displayed in a Marrakesh salon, yard goods for sale in the Chaouen souk.

The unusual wool wall hangings and rugs above were designed by textile collector Bert Flint. Spools of fine silk are sold in the Fez souk. A living room outside of Essaouira is decorated with traditional fabrics. Costumed stick figures are displayed by women during a festival in Marrakesh.

needleworkers often opted for cotton or wool threads of brilliant reds, yellows, and purples.

Today, it is in interior design where the use of textiles in Morocco is being rethought. There is movement toward a more livable, relaxed look, especially in Marrakesh. Both in the medina and outside town, homeowners are using traditional country textiles for bedspreads, curtains, and upholstery. They prowl souks in search of colorful striped Berber wools from the mountains near Chaouen; off-white, nubbly, couscous-textured cottons from Essaouira; and rough-textured wools and cottons in a desert-toned brown from Taroudant.

OPPOSITE: Moroccan textiles worn as clothing frequently clash in pattern and color. ABOVE: inspiration for colors in Moroccan fabrics is found in the country's infinite variety of wildflowers, which are frequently found in bundles of fresh-cut grass used to feed livestock.

# Rugs

FOR HUNDREDS OF YEARS AMID the cedar forests and snowbound valleys of the Atlas Mountains, in the shadow of crenellated walls of Saharan kasbahs, and along the labyrinthian alleyways of urban medinas, Moroccan women have woven rugs.

Appreciated for their exciting color combinations and often distinctive designs, Moroccan rugs are divided into two categories: rural and urban. Rural rugs are further identified by region, then by tribe (of which there are over five hundred in Morocco). For the

**ABOVE: a vendor in Essaouira shows wool yarn to a potential buyer. RIGHT: ask to see a rug and you'll be shown a hundred at the Bazaar du Sud in Marrakesh.**

most part, rural rugs are striped, although stylized motifs inspired by ancient symbols or strong imaginations are not uncommon. Rugs from Rehamna and Chiadma are as abstract as paintings by Jackson Pollock or Piet Mondrian; they are especially prized for their distinctive weave and colors that range from subtle earth tones to brilliant saffrons, beryls, and crimsons.

Urban rugs are made mainly in

**OPPOSITE: in Fez, wool dyeing has been done by hand—and by feet—for hundreds of years by the same families in the souk. ABOVE LEFT: white wool yarn will be turned into a thick pile rug at a weaving collective in Sidi-Moktar. All-white rugs are mainly exported to Europe. ABOVE: synthetic dyes are popular today and produce rugs with colors verging on neon. LEFT: on "Throne Day" the king and his entourage will drive over these Rabat rugs spread out on the streets of Marrakesh.**

Rabat and Mediouna and have a more formal design than rural carpets. Easily recognizable by their palette of vivid oranges, sunset reds, spring greens, and soft mauves, they frequently have a large center field covered with octagonal medallions. Motifs include flowers, teapots, toads, palm trees, and mules.

Berber rugs have strong geometric designs and often combine thick pile and flat weave. Less expensive, though popular with folk art collectors, are Berber mats. These are woven from dwarf palm or esperato grass with decorative designs woven into them in wool most often in shades of red.

**ABOVE: wool for rugmaking hangs from a loom. OPPOSITE: on chilly winter days, rug merchants curl up in their inventory to keep warm.**

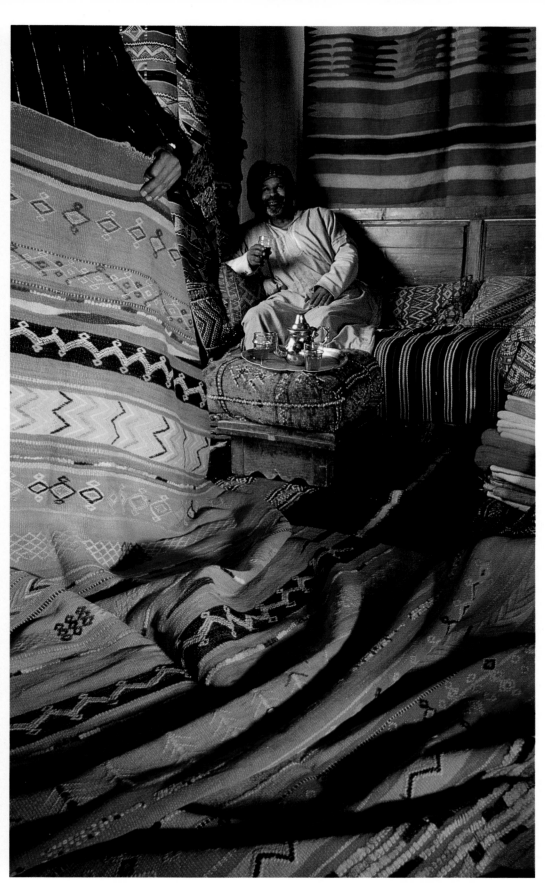

OPPOSITE:
less expensive
and increasingly
appreciated, Berber rugs
made out of dwarf palm
or esperato grass
reproduce decorative
designs popular in wool.
Long uncut vegetable
fibers along their backs
serve as a natural
cushion. These rugs also
cover walls for winter
warmth. CENTER: fringe
on many contemporary
rugs is often simply the
result of weavers leaving
floating waft threads
uncut. LEFT: a merchant
displays rugs for sale at
the Bazaar du Sud in
Marrakesh.

Almost all Moroccan rugs are stamped by government officials with color-coded labels for quality. The wool used must be spun from fleece and the colors made from colorfast dyes. As for value: "We look for the originality of the weaver," explains Moulay Charif, owner of the well-known Bazaar du Sud rug store in Marrakesh. "Repetition of design in a rug lowers the price. Spontaneity and creativity in weaving raises it." When selling, weavers turn to runners working the countryside or sell directly at a rug auction.

Shoppers with sufficient stamina may test their mettle at a rug shop, where multiple rounds of mint tea will accompany the fifty, seventy-five, even as many as one hundred rugs spread out at one's feet. Experienced buyers counsel that one must bargain hard, beware of nylon threads passing for silk, and deal only with reputable shopkeepers. *Caveat emptor.*

**BELOW: rare antique Berber rugs are appreciated for the many symbolic patterns and designs woven into them. OPPOSITE: like abstract paintings, Berber rugs, such as this one in the Bert Flint collection, are often nonrepresentational.**

# Leather

WITH THE RETURN OF THE MOORS
from Spain in the 15th century,
Fez became the center of the
leather industry. The expertise of
its tanners and bookbinders made
the word "Morocco" synony-
mous throughout the Western
world with fine leather. Still
today, Fez is the center of the Moroccan leather industry.

Visitors to Fez climb up slip-
pery, narrow stairs in Dabbaghin,
the section of the souk where the
tanneries are located. From roof-
tops, and holding bouquets of
mint to minimize the awful
stench, they look down upon a
medieval scene. Hundreds of men
stand calf-deep in honeycombed
vats full of chemical dyes and cow
urine—only a few tanneries continue to use bark and plant pig-
ments. The workers' bare legs

OPPOSITE: in Fez,
cowhides, camelskins,
and goatskins are
spread out to dry after
dyeing. LEFT, FROM
TOP: skins are washed,
scraped, and soaked
for several days to
soften them. Leather is
often painted after it is
dyed. What isn't
exported or turned into
*babouches* may be sold
in the souk.

vary in color from yellow, red, and blue to green and black—the result of treading on cowhides, goatskins, and camelskins for up to twelve hours a day.

The finished skins are rubbed with wooden blocks to remove wrinkles, dried in the sun, and then stacked and tied in bunches according to size and quality. Moroccan leather is a multimillion-dollar export. What remains in the country is turned into *babouches* (hand-embroidered slippers), hassocks, bags, belts, and saddles.

**Yellow *babouches* are traditional Moroccan leather slippers worn by men.**

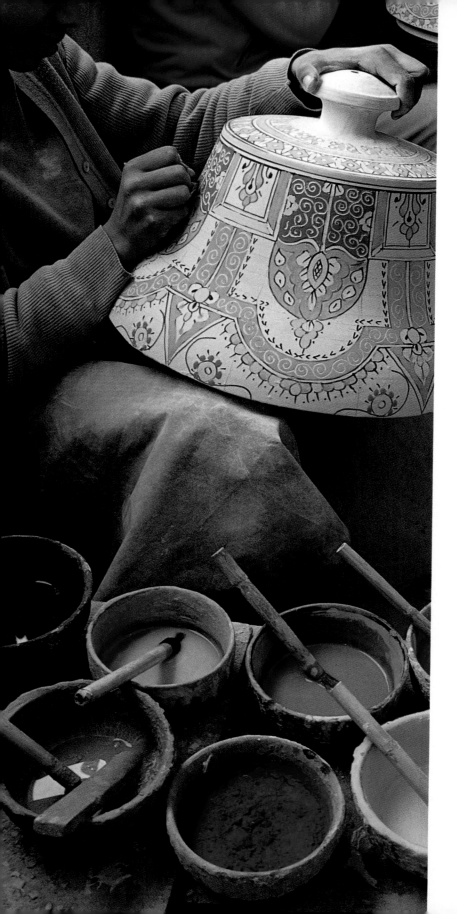

# Pottery

THE HISTORY OF MOROCCAN pottery dates back a thousand years. However, it was in the 15th century when the craft truly became important. Moors skilled in pottery fled Spain for Morocco and settled in Fez, Meknes, Safi, and Marrakesh. Here they rebuilt their kilns. And for the next four centuries, Moroccan potters, particularly those in Fez, prospered and produced some of the finest examples of their trade in the Islamic world.

By the beginning of the 20th century, however, the quality of Moroccan pottery had diminished. The importation of mass-produced pottery from Europe reduced the incentive of Moroccan potters to practice their skills.

A renaissance of the centuries-old Moroccan pottery industry

**LEFT: a worker applies the design to a jar in the pottery kiln in Safi. OPPOSITE: Yves Saint Laurent and Pierre Berge use this whimsical 1920s jar with a palm tree motif as a doorstop in their house in Marrakesh.**

OPPOSITE: in Safi, 1920s-style vases are made for export. Their simplicity and strong colors are popular in Europe. LEFT, FROM TOP: Moroccan potters soften clay by foot before shaping it by hand. Roof tiles are dyed by hand. Jars wait to be fired in a kiln in Safi.

occurred during the French Protectorate. Anxious to introduce Moroccan craftsmanship to the European market, the resident-general, Louis Lyautey, sent Moroccan potters to Sèvres in France to learn new techniques. Examples of their rekindled skill were introduced at the Fez Fair in 1916. The local as well as European markets were quick to support the new work.

Today, thousands of Moroccan

**ABOVE LEFT: a Saharan water jar decorates the entrance to a private house in the medina in Marrakesh. ABOVE: a worker at the Safi kilns carries clay. LEFT: a jar is nestled in a blanket for display.**

Pottery is displayed
at dozens of street stalls
that line the street
leading to the Safi kilns.

potters pound clay, spin wheels, and shape the myriad bowls, vases, and dishes that continue to be made in the country's historic pottery centers.

Traditional Andalusian-inspired, polychrome enameled pottery made in Fez is the most respected in Morocco. It is blue and white for the most part, though yellow, green, white, black, and brown glazes are also common. Fez pottery dinner plates, *jebana*, or butter jars, carafes, pitchers, vases, perfume jars, and inkstands are found in shops throughout the country.

Fakhkhari Hamida et Fils is a major pottery workshop on the outskirts of Fez. Here the division of labor continues in the same way it has in the pottery trade for centuries. A dozen young male apprentices race from station to station, carrying different items to the older men who spin the potting wheels and stoke and pack

the kilns. At this particular workshop, women design and trace intricate traditional Islamic patterns onto the pieces of pottery.

Pottery buffs also enjoy visiting Safi to see the country's oldest kilns. Located on Potters' Hill, they are more than two hundred years old and still in operation. Here, potters produce fanciful, repetitive designs on turquoise, white, and cream-colored backgrounds.

Polychrome glazed pottery

OPPOSITE: two 19th-century Fez polychromed enamel dishes rest against a painted 19th-century wood panel. ABOVE: roof tiles are laid out to dry in the sun.

made in Meknes is the most widely distributed in Morocco. It is sold in souks and at roadside stands everywhere.

Unlike Europe, where many ceramics were made for decoration and to show off the skill of their makers, Moroccan pottery has always been utilitarian. This explains why so many pieces of Moroccan pottery are nicked and chipped. It also explains why there are so few genuine antique pieces of Moroccan pottery in existence today.

*Rahalia*, large Moroccan plates from Fez, made strictly for wall decoration, are an exception; many are truly old. So are decorated Saharan and Berber terra-cotta ware: olive oil jugs, milk and water pots, oil lamps, teapots, and animal figures. Like all examples of fine Moroccan pottery, they, too, are now sought by collectors worldwide.

**FROM TOP: a street sign directs customers to "Potters' Hill" in Safi. Written in Arabic and French, the sign summarizes the recent history of Morocco. Nineteenth-century *jebanas*, or butter pots, are occasionally found in antique shops. Rimmed in copper to prevent them from chipping, bichrome bowls are made by Fakhkhari Hamida et Fils in Fez. OPPOSITE: a shipment of antiques for export to a retail outlet in Santa Fe, New Mexico, includes oil storage jars from Taroudant.**

120

# Thuya Wood

THUYA TREES RESEMBLE SCRUB oaks and are native to the flat, sandy countryside outside Essaouira on the Atlantic shoreline. The short, scruffy trees are valued for the extraordinary beauty of their wood, which ranges in color from dark mahogany brown to subtle buff. Thuya may be all one color, all one grain; or it may be burled, with an explosion of grains and varying hues.

The popularity of thuya reached its height during the French Protectorate. And because many Europeans were living in Morocco, thuya bureaus, armoires, tables, and chairs made there in the early 20th century reflected European taste.

**Danish designer, collector, and gallery owner Frederick Damgaard restored a 150-year-old house in Essaouira. He entertains friends at his antique mother-of-pearl and thuya wood dining room tables.**

Today, hundreds of wood-workers in Essaouira spend twelve-hour days inside ateliers under miles of arcades that line the narrow streets of the blue-shut-tered, all-white seaport. Skilled in marquetry, they finalize their handicrafts by rubbing the boxes, chess sets, tables, chairs, picture frames, and jewelry for hours with small cotton balls soaked in vegetable oil, bringing out the wood's patina. Workshop en-trances are piled high with thuya wood ready to be worked. And dozens of crates of finished items wait for delivery to Moroccan souks or shipment abroad.

# Casablanca Deco

WHAT NEW YORK CITY IS TO THE UNITED STATES, CASABLANCA IS to Morocco: a crowded, noisy, wealthy, commercial center on the Atlantic coast. The North African metropolis is surprisingly unappreciated, both at home and abroad, for its unique abundance of Art Deco architecture. ✋ Once a sleepy, out-of-the-way fishing village, Casablanca blossomed under the French Protectorate and became a boom town with a first-class port. Along its wide, palm-lined boulevards luxurious Art Deco apartment and office buildings reminiscent of the Trocadero district in Paris sprang up. ✋ Today, Casablanca city officials are anxious to establish an Art Deco historic district. Efforts are under way to rekindle public appreciation of the city's dazzling collection of building facades, front doors, balconies, and balustraded staircases from the increasingly popular 1920s and 1930s.

Downtown Casablanca attracts apartment dwellers who want to live in Art Deco buildings with fanciful, all-white facades and wrought-iron balconies.

Rhythmic Art Deco designs
with floral, bird, animal, and
abstract geometric
motifs, influenced by European
and Islamic traditions, are seen
throughout Casablanca.
Art Deco wrought-iron windows,
staircases, and balconies—
as well as stuccoed
pediments and friezes—
punctuate the city.

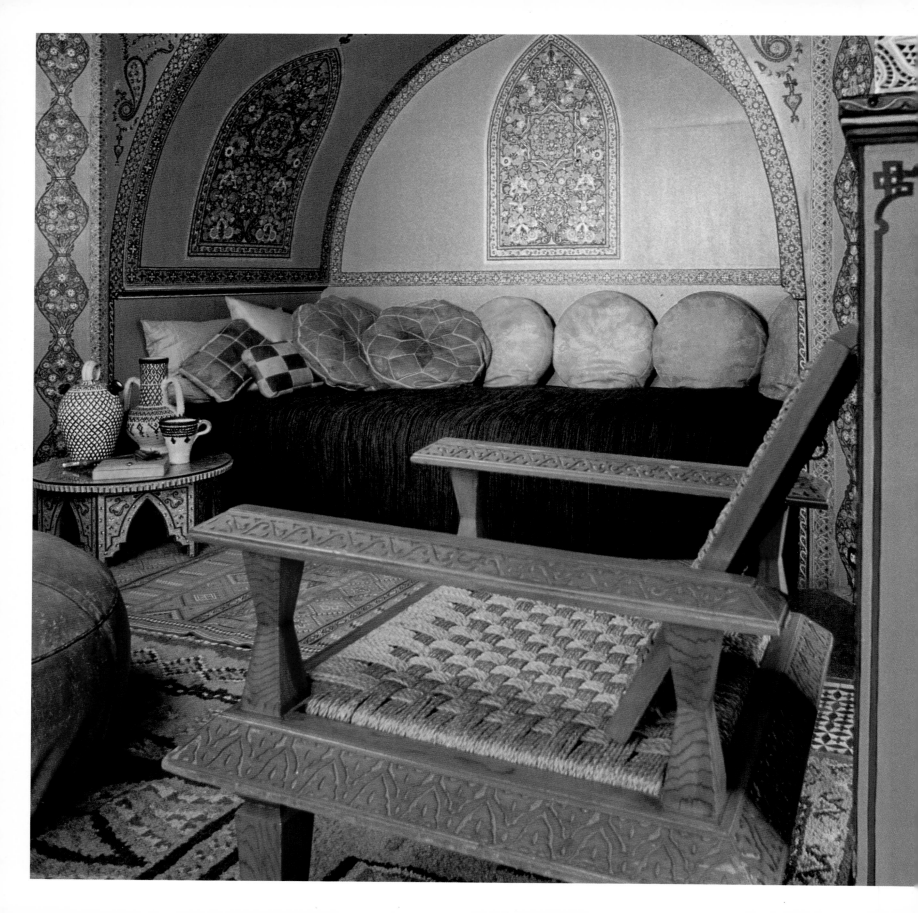

# Landmark Villa

HOME FOR MORE THAN SIXTY YEARS OF THE LEGENDARY COUNTESS de Breteuil, the Hispano-Moorish Villa Taylor is in the middle of Marrakesh yet hidden from public view. It lies today behind massive, guarded gates in an enormous garden of palm, fir, and olive trees. ✋ A superb example of lavish, massive, pre–World War II Moroccan architecture and interior design—the house was built in the 1920s —the villa's huge main rooms contain museum-quality handpainted ceilings, doors, and shutters. "Scholars come here all the time to study the craftsmanship," says the countess. ✋ With many cozy, secluded small rooms in towers up hidden staircases, perfect for têtes-à-têtes or *liaisons amoureuses*, the villa is best known for the splendor and richness of its Moroccan-tiled living room, where visitors step back in time. Tigerskin rugs, deep sofas piled with pillows covered in

131

Moroccan fabrics, big leather ottomans, a shortwave radio picking up jazz beamed in from Paris, tables crowded with family photographs in silver frames and vases of pink and red roses from the garden: *le grand salon* is a marvelous continuation of French Protectorate *luxe* life-style in Morocco. Here, for years, the countess has entertained scores of friends beneath a towering, sumptuous green-and-yellow Marrakesh-style wood ceiling. Painted with *zwags*, floral and geometric motifs, it is made—as is all paneling in Morocco—from rotproof and wormproof Atlas Mountain

FAR LEFT: a massive front door opens onto a foyer. ABOVE LEFT: a brass door bell is placed in the center of a hand of Fatima—a talisman against the evil eye. LEFT AND OPPOSITE: in the *grand salon*, under an enormous painted wood ceiling, hangs an 18th-century ancestor portrait of Gabrielle Emilie de Breteuil, Marquise du Chatalet.

cedar, which doesn't need to be treated or varnished. True to tradition, the lower part of the wall is covered with a panel of *zelliges*, the upper portion with a frieze of very finely carved plaster of Paris windows, or *chems*.

An ancient bell system still serves a purpose in the rambling three-story villa. When the signal under the word "Madame" flashes, it usually signifies that it is time to take the countess her breakfast tray. Bells labeled "Chambre Rouge," "Chambre Jaune," and "Chambre Bleu" summon the staff to eight guest rooms, each with a different Moroccan motif, a sunken marble bathtub, well-worn rugs, and a fireplace. "Loge" is the wood-paneled card room. And "Secret" (for "*Secrétaire*") is the library, where Winston Churchill and Franklin Roosevelt sat down for further talks after the Casablanca

**Painted wood doors are juxtaposed with multicolored tiles in a guest bedroom. The different types of craftsmanship throughout Villa Taylor are superb examples of the numerous decorative elements found in private houses and palaces in Morocco.**

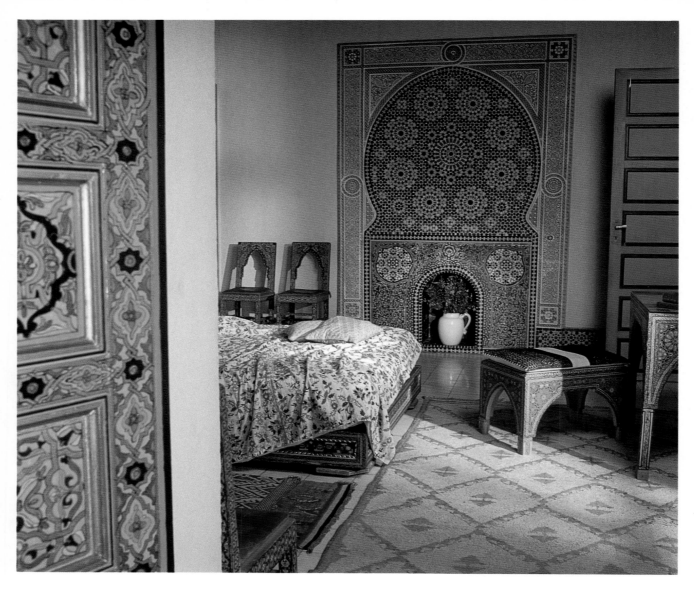

ABOVE: different color
themes give identity
to the villa's guest
rooms. RIGHT: breakfast
trays await delivery by
the staff each morning
in the courtyard.

136

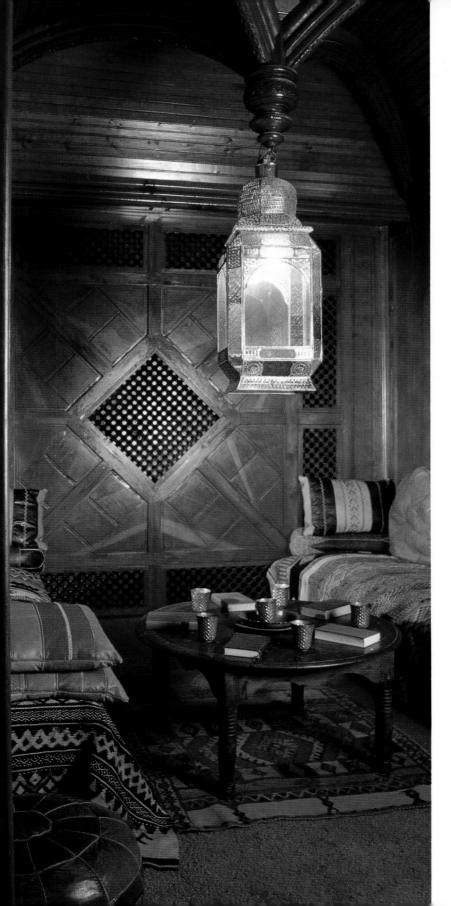

Conference in January of 1943.

"Churchill was so moved by the sight of the snow-capped Atlas from the villa roof, he persuaded the president to allow himself to be taken out of his wheelchair and carried up," the countess recalls. "It was dusk. The mountains were blood red and the muezzins had begun to call the faithful to prayer. It was one of the deepest moments in the two friends' lives."

Today, the Countess de Breteuil climbs the same three staircases up to her roof several times a day, alone. From morning until evening, she has never grown tired of her view. *"C'est ma promenade,"* she says, and smiles.

**Unpainted wood, seen in this jewel-like cedar *petit salon* inset with *moucharaby* panels, is uncommon in Morocco. Rural weavings and leather pillows give a Saharan atmosphere to the room.**

# A Moroccan Folly

U.S. AMBASSADOR TO MOROCCO FREDERICK VREELAND, AND HIS wife, artist Vanessa Somers, once lived in Rome. But they vacationed in Marrakesh, where they have built, are still building, and insist they will always be building Villa Cafrevan in the Palmeraie, or palm oasis. Inside and out, it is a blend of Indian, Moroccan, Italian, and 1001 Nights architecture whose unconventionality has amazed all of Marrakesh for years. ✋ The rambling, adobe fun house, designed by French solar architect Dominic Michelis, is multileveled and contains endless grand salons, petits salons, nooks, crannies, grottoes, staircases, landings, hideaways, and balconies. There are eight theme bedrooms—Jungle, Bonsai, Nursery, and Tantra among them—and twelve baths. ✋ Surrounded by acres of palms, umbrella pines from Italy, litchi trees from China, and mango trees from Florida, the villa's first non-Moroccan surprise is a columned entryway. It is a replica of Borromini's famed trompe l'oeil loggia in the Palazzo Spada in Rome. "Vanessa and I don't take ourselves seriously. We love things that fool the eye, that have humor, that show a bit of eccentricity," Vreeland explains.

The villa's exterior definitely lives up to its two owners' whimsical, eclectic demands. There are Moghul-style cupolas, chimneys, and windows copied from the fa-

ABOVE: domes and chimneys on the roof were inspired by the 16th-century city of Fatephur Sikri in India. OPPOSITE: Marble and glass mosaics were ordered in Carrara and Murano for Villa Cafrevan's upper terrace swimming pool designed by Vanessa Somers.

RIGHT: different colors of adobe were used on a new tumbled-down, crosshatched wall made to look old. "We like anything that fools the eye," Vreeland says. OPPOSITE: grillwork covers Moghul-style windows. Heavy outside canvas curtains with black leather trim are copies of an ancient Roman design. Flanked by 16th-century Spanish columns is a *coin de repas,* or eating alcove; a 19th-century Kashmiri shawl covers the table. The villa's eclectic architecture includes a Moroccan brick arch, which frames a nearby palm tree.

ABOVE: colorful scraps
of fabric decorate straw
mats. RIGHT: striped
canvas chairs, off-white
umbrellas, and Berber
straw mats are spread
around the swimming
pool each morning and
returned to the pool
room each evening.

bled city of Fatehpur Sikri in India; purposely half-ruined adobe walls with white checkerboard design are reminiscent of Moroccan kasbahs; heavy white canvas caidal-style curtains hang in doorways.

A protégé of Professor Odoardo Anselmi, head of the Vatican School of Mosaics, Somers designed the villa's swimming pool and personally laid thousands of Murano glass and Carrara marble mosaics at the bottom. Shimmering beneath the surface is an Italo-Moroccan landscape reminiscent of the work of Claude Lorrain.

# A Former Harem

AN AMERICAN FROM MISSISSIPPI, DESIGNER BILL WILLIS MOVED TO Morocco from Europe, where he worked in the 1960s. ✋ Among the first foreigners to settle deep in the Marrakesh medina, Willis bought and restored Dar Noujoun, House of the Stars, on the Rue Sebaatourigel. The harem of a royal palace, it is next to an Arab cemetery where the stern warning *Interdit Aux Non Muslemans* ("Forbidden to Non-Moslems") is painted forbiddingly on a crumbling wall. ✋ Known for his skill in adapting traditional high-style Hispano-Moorish architecture to Western tastes, the multitalented expatriate triggered a revival. Over the last twenty years, he has designed new and restored old properties throughout Marrakesh for a roster of clients that includes the Paul Gettys, Alain Delon, Yves Saint Laurent and Pierre Berge, and Marie-Hélène de Rothschild. He

147

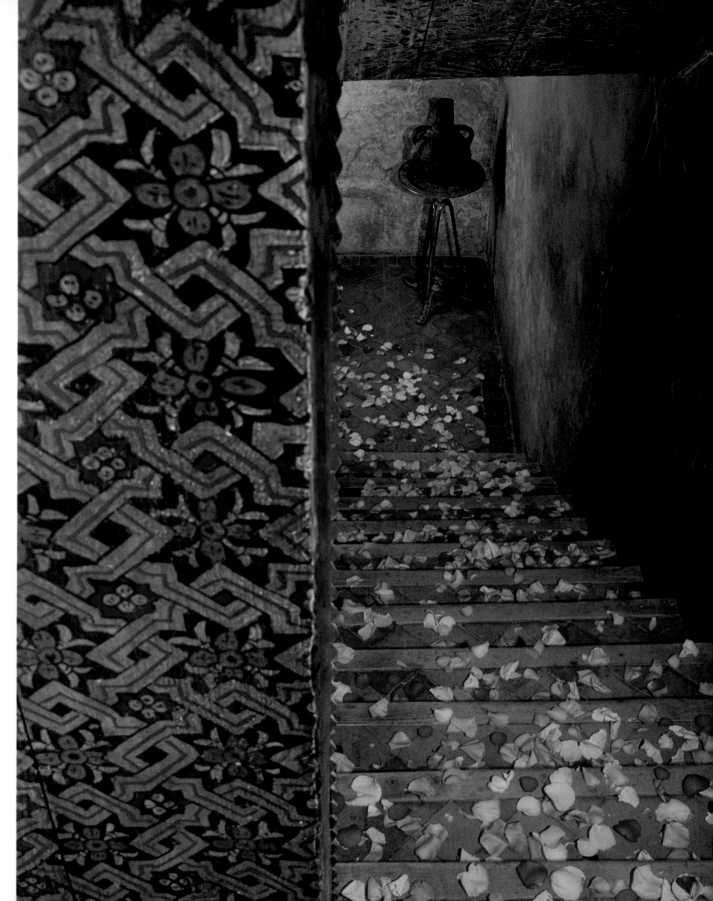

A narrow staircase
containing a bronze
table and Berber
pot leads from the ground-
floor entrance hall
up to the reception rooms
on the second floor. For
parties, the staircase
is scattered with
rose petals.

also serves as design consultant to members of the royal family of Morocco.

Entered through a nondescript alley and up an inside stair with risers of glazed blue, black, and yellow tiles, Willis's own retreat is well known to hundreds of visitors to Morocco. Round-the-clock invitations to lunch, dinner, or cocktails allow friends and friends of friends to see one of the

ABOVE LEFT: an arrangement of roses fills a ceramic pot on a Moroccan rug. ABOVE: a 1st-century Roman bronze foot, a 17th-century Malasian *kreiss*, or dagger, and a 17th-century English embroidered box join forces on a 19th-century inlaid Moroccan table. LEFT: in Willis's old rose-colored living room, Renaissance bronze fire dogs add drama to his *tadelakt* and tile fireplace.

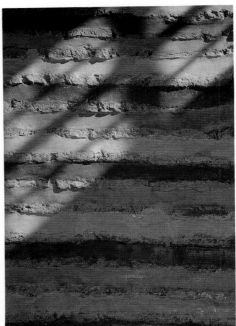

most superb restorations of a residence in Morocco.

First-time viewers are immediately struck by the house's fanciful Moroccan tile fireplaces and shiny *tadelakt* walls, both Willis trademarks. Originally used in *hammams*, or baths, *tadelakt* is a Moroccan wall treatment that combines plaster, sand, and natural coloring, polished to a high sheen with smooth stones and hand soap.

*Tadelakt* walls in oxblood, rust, gray, tan, and yellow are especially popular in Marrakesh. But

OPPOSITE: a long, narrow corridor with brick and *tadelakt* walls and floors of Moroccan tiles leads to the dining room and kitchen. LEFT: Willis often serves tea in his library. The mantel above his *tadelakt* and brick fireplace holds two 18th-century Moroccan vases and a 16th-century Turkish mortar.

151

RIGHT: a Moroccan-style *faux marbre* lantern sits on top of 19th-century Chinese fabric. BELOW: walls of exposed brick and tricolor *tadelakt* lend dramatic dimension to a fluted chimney in the dining room. An open-work opium table sits in an alcove behind an Afghan curtain; the embroidery on the pillow was commissioned and made in Marrakesh.

A maze of rooms and hallways, the house contains museum-quality 18th- and 19th-century painted wooden doors and carved wooden panels. *Moucharaby*, traditional turned wood in a mesh design, can serve to filter the harsh, hot sunlight.

153

Willis's acclaimed courage with color extends to the aubergine, turquoise, mustard, crimson, navy blue, and green trim that outlines several doors along an entrance hall. The hall leads to a living room lit by candles at night, scented with sandalwood, and filled with Moroccan and European antiques. "When I first saw the room, which is twenty by twenty foot, I was amazed to realize it was square, not long and narrow like most Moroccan rooms. It was enough to make me buy the house," Willis recalls.

In the dining room, exposed layers of very thin bricks are alternate shades of mustard, burgundy, and beige. A dining table at Western height reveals Willis's refusal to sit cross-legged on the floor Moroccan-style. "I did it for years, but I'm back to my old American ways," he admits. "Tradition is fine, but it is comfort that counts."

**In the master bedroom, an Iranian kilim hangs over a bed covered with a Bukhara embroidered spread and a Moroccan embroidered pillow. A pair of 1925 armchairs upholstered with contemporary Afghan kilims flanks a table covered with an Afghan tablecloth.**

# Thé à la Menthe

THE OFFER OF A GLASS OF MINT TEA IS AS MUCH A PART OF SOCIAL behavior in Morocco as wine is in France. Traditional, expected, never refused, mint tea is served when people first meet, constantly when they are together, and when they prepare to say good-bye. The Moroccan tea ceremony is in fact a ritual as carefully defined as the Japanese one. ✋ After a few pinches of tea are sprinkled into a metal teapot, boiling water is added. A hefty bunch of mint leaves is then stuffed into the pot and allowed to steep. Lumps of sugar—cut from a conical loaf covered with purple paper and bought in the souk—are the last ingredient. ✋ Twice a glass of tea is poured, then returned to the pot. Finally, the brew is ready for drinking. The server then raises the pot several feet away from a metal tray of small decorated glasses and pours quickly. He never misses his mark.

**Introduced to Morocco by the British in the mid-19th century, tea quickly became the nation's favorite drink. Sprigs of fresh mint and lots of sugar are customary additives.**

157

ABOVE: cafés are frequented mostly by men, who spend hours gossiping, smoking, and drinking endless glasses of tea. RIGHT: in the terrace café adjacent to the Andalusian gardens of the Museum of Moroccan Arts in Rabat, a 19th-century tea stove continues to be used daily.

**ABOVE:** fresh mint is mandatory for making tea in Morocco. **RIGHT:** at the hotel Gazelle d'Or in Taroudant, a very elaborate service is used to make *thé à la menthe* that is served to guests after dinner.

# The Souk

*"BALEK, BALEK!"* "MAKE WAY, MAKE WAY!" ✋ CRIES ARE HEARD as mule trains weave through souks, or markets, in every small village and large town in Morocco. They are all things to all people. A labyrinth of small shops, a souk is boutique, flea market, recycling center, supermarket, department store, open-air reception with receiving line, circus, sideshow, and mob scene all at the same time. ✋ Shaded by loose reed mat "ceilings" that slash the air with dusty shadows and bright bars of scorching sunlight, the serpentine alleys and dead ends of a souk are lined with shops, each with its own specialty: rugs, copperware, furniture, kitchenware, silk tassels, herbal medicines, slippers, and antique windows and doors. ✋ Burlap bags overflow with cardamom, cumin, and coriander. There are mounds of mint, pickled olives, and dates. Wooden crates spill over

ABOVE: for centuries, donkeys have carried merchandise in and out of the narrow lanes in souks. RIGHT: Berber jewelry and a *jebana* await sale in the souk in Taroudant. OPPOSITE: even chickens are available in the souk.

162

with citrus. Fresh loaves of bread are stacked up like poker chips. Clothing racks dip low from the weight of men's *djellabas* and *burnooses* and women's caftans.

The souk in Fez is the oldest, most medieval, most replete with traditional Moroccan handicrafts. With the largest selection of fine rugs, antique Berber jewelry, and pots from the Sahara, the souk in Marrakesh is the most frenzied and most touristy.

The Marrakesh souk also offers a good deal more than shopping. Here each evening, entertainers turn the Place Djemaa El Fna into one of the greatest shows on earth. Sorcerers, comedians, story-tellers, wrestlers, boxers, snake charmers, and acrobats join forces to produce a ten-ring circus, one that has been going on daily for centuries. "In the beginning," it is said, "there was the Djemaa El Fna."

**RIGHT:** Shop signs such as this gigantic flounder outside a seafood store are common. The hand of Fatima averts the evil eye.
**OVERLEAF:** Moroccan women shop daily in the thousands of souks for everything from food to cosmetics. Newsprint often serves as wrapping, and in the country, there are even "parking lots" for donkeys. Vendors expect that bargaining will play a part in each transaction, whether it be for a woven basket or the dried rose petals displayed in a basket.

OPPOSITE: donkey saddles, woven bread baskets, pottery, and Berber jewelry: contemporary folk art as well as antique handicrafts are for sale in a souk. LEFT: deep-fried doughnuts are strung on a grass reed for a hungry buyer.

ABOVE: woven Berber bread baskets from around Marrakesh await export from the souk to New Mexico. RIGHT: men gossip and haggle over prices in the souk in Tafrout.

# Decorative Arts

A painter completes work on a ceiling panel commissioned in his workshop in the Fez souk. When it is finished, it will be taken to the house and installed.

THE FIRST-TIME VISITOR TO MOROCCO MAY BE DAZZLED BY THE colorful and courageous combinations of tiles, plasterwork, and painted surfaces on walls, doors, shutters, ceilings, and floors in private houses and hotels as well as in the arches and on pathways leading into buildings. But Moroccans have traditionally relied on the decoration of walls, ceilings, and floors to "furnish" a house. ✋ A proverb explains why Moroccans have always made the courtyards, reception rooms, and living areas of their homes rich in ornate details. They are adherents of the belief that "the first thing one should own is a home; and it is the last thing one should sell, for a home is one's tomb this side of heaven." This combines with the belief of Abu 'Inan, a 14th-century homeowner: "That which is beautiful is not dear at any cost, and that which pleases man cannot be too expensive."

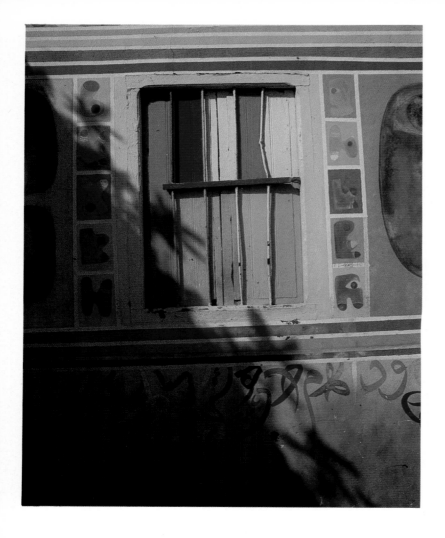

# Painted Surfaces

MOROCCANS ARE MASTERS OF painted wood and gypsum, or plaster of Paris, surfaces. Following the Prophet's command not to depict humans, they paint trees, elaborate and stylized flower bouquets, ingeniously varied motifs of sinuous vines, leaf-shaped arabesques, and inanimate objects. Ornate, colorful, abstract Islamic designs with strong mathematical symmetry are rendered by artists who seek to transport viewers into a state of uplifted thought.

Berber painters too are adept at painting on wood. Rich in symbolism and conveying ancient mystical messages, Berber painted surfaces are abstract; and because Berbers are less likely to adhere to the strictures of Islamic design, their painted surfaces are a great deal more personal and often

**ABOVE LEFT: calligraphy in bright colors decorates the exteriors of buildings in Asilah, a fishing village on the Atlantic seacoast. LEFT: elaborate repeated motifs are worked in paint on gypsum. OPPOSITE: Mustapha Boumazzourh, a sculptor, designed and painted a contemporary Moroccan motif on a door at his 19th-century Essaouira farmhouse.**

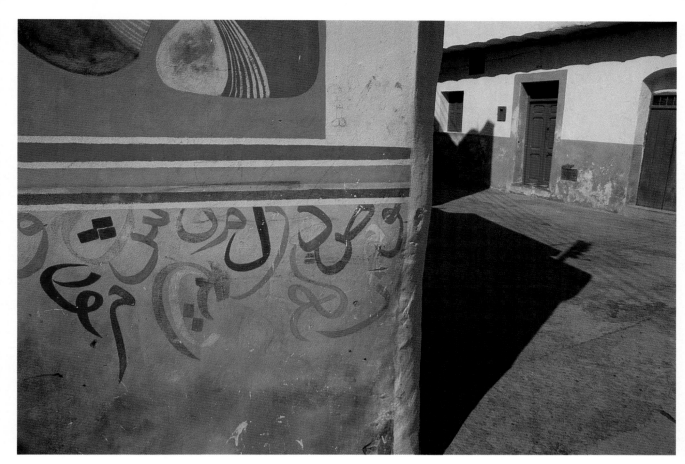

combine unexpected colors.

Firm believers that a wooden piece is not finished until it is covered with decorations, Moroccan homeowners and designers keep the country's *zawwaga*, or painters on wood, in heavy demand. Each job is different. Like their ancestors, Moroccan *zawwaga* today spend weeks, even months, working on wooden cupolas, alcoves, doors, and ceilings in private houses and new hotels.

Like all skilled craftsmen and artisans in Morocco, painters work under a *maallem*, or master craftsman. Some stand up while painting; others sit cross-legged. They hold their brushes, which are made out of hair from donkey tails, vertically, their wrists supported by their left hands to allow fingers to be completely supple.

Colors are applied first; the out-

**OPPOSITE: a painted door to the restaurant Yacout in Marrakesh opens onto a corridor laid with brick-shaped tiles from Fez. ABOVE: many painters decorate town walls and doors along the narrow streets of Asilah during the annual summer arts festival.**

lines that emphasize contours come later. To the distress of purists, the natural, vibrant egg-yolk-based colors of the past reminiscent of the brilliance seen in medieval manuscripts have given way to the strident colors of modern-day chemical paints.

Workers in gypsum or plaster of Paris are equally respected in Morocco for their technical and artistic skills. After a specialist has drawn endlessly repeated motifs of squares, circles, triangles, stylized stars, almonds, flowers, even scallop shells, plasterwork artists, or *ghabbar*, carve reliefs in four or five layers, both on the surface of a wall and in hollowed-out details that vary in depth.

Plaster of Paris in Morocco is either left its natural eggshell color or polychromed in vibrant primary colors.

**OPPOSITE: a painted chair designed by Yves Saint Laurent sits on an Agadir marble floor in the foyer of his Marrakesh villa. The painted walls and door date to the 1930s and 40s, when painter Jacques Majorelle lived in the house. LEFT, FROM TOP: Berber-inspired herringbone twig-and-beam painted ceilings in the Moroccan-style Tishka Hotel. Intricately decorated polychrome gypsum detail in a private house in Marrakesh. Brightly colored Berber living room ceiling boards.**

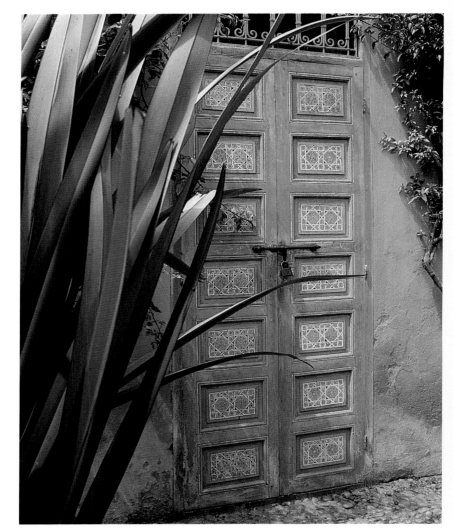

RIGHT: this handpainted late 19th-century door is one of many surrounding the garden courtyard at the Museum of Moroccan Arts in Rabat. BELOW RIGHT: the Mediterranean villa of Madame Sete Guetta in Cabo Negro contains superb examples of early 19th-century painted furniture from nearby Tetouan.
OPPOSITE: a 19th-century Berber ceiling from the Bert Flint collection in Marrakesh. Berber houses are decorated with warm colors and geometric designs, both whimsical and symbolic.

*Ghabbar*, or master artisans of gypsum, carve decorative reliefs that may be left a natural eggshell color or polychromed in rich vibrant hues. The scallop wall panel at left is from the sultan's palace in Tangier.

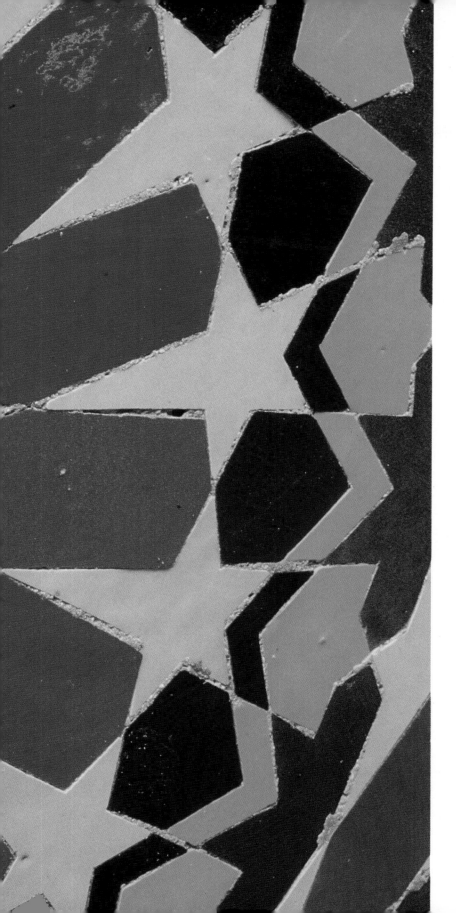

# Tiles

DECORATIVE AS WELL AS STRUCtural and architectural, Moroccan handmade tiles are among the most colorful in the world. Derived from Byzantine and Roman mosaics, *zelliges*, or wall tiles, are Morocco's great specialty, both in the skill with which they are made and because of the expertise with which they are laid. Traditionally, they have been used for inside decoration in wall panels, staircases, archways, and columns. Today, foreign designers order *zelliges* to be made in their own colors and shapes and use them in tables, fireplaces, picture frames, even chairs.

Moroccan tile production has long been centered in Fez. Adhering to the centuries-old process, local clay is thrown into basins carved in the ground and is then

French architect Michel Pinseau has designed the Hassan II mosque in Casablanca. Many interior walls are covered with Moroccan tiles exhibiting a modern approach to traditional Islamic design. The pentacle and crescent moon, the national emblem of Morocco, is the central motif in this tile panel.

Wall tiles in the Saadian
tombs, built in
Marrakesh by Ahmed
Edh Dhahabi at the end
of the 16th century,
are elaborately patterned.

mixed with water. After a twenty-four-hour stabilizing period, an *ajjan*, or mixer, kneads the clay. He eliminates any stones, bits of wood, or other foreign elements. Next, a *fakhkhar*, or workman, molds the clay into rectangular slabs that are dried in the sun, coated with different colored glazes, and fired. The ovens are heated with wood, grasses, and crushed olive pits, and the temperature inside will reach eight hundred degrees.

The unique aspect of making *zelliges* begins next. A designer traces the outline of the pieces to be cut out of the tile slab. He makes his design with an *ud el khizran*, or bamboo stick, dipped in ink. Andre Paccard displays more than 350 different shapes and sizes in his book *Traditional Islamic Craft in Moroccan Architecture*. Some are so small, 150 can fit on a matchbook cover.

ABOVE LEFT: designer Bill Willis sought to update and give new direction to traditional Islamic design in the tile fireplaces and furnishings of the Tishka Hotel in Marrakesh. LEFT: with bases of plaster of Paris, columns in the courtyard of the Palais Mokri in Fez are covered with traditional *zelliges*, or tiles. The stained glass in the window was imported from Italy.

The final and most delicate step is the actual cutting out of the *zelliges* from the slab. This is the work of a *taksir*, or tile cutter, who uses a hammer that has been sharpened on both sides. Filed smooth and sorted according to shape, size, and color, the *zelliges* are then taken to the job site and laid into patterns by a *maallem*.

Traditional patterns, with such evocative names as hen's feet, divided tears, little tambourine, and heifer's eyes, are most common. But contemporary adaptations of traditional Islamic designs are beginning to be introduced. Regardless, the patterns must always conform to the Islamic geometric grid. The result is that Moroccan tile designs cannot be judged by the originality of the design but by the combinations of colors and the flair with which the *maallem* has depicted crescents, triangles, stars, lozenges, and squares.

**LEFT: detail of tiles designed by Bill Willis for his fireplace in Marrakesh. The *ferragha*, or layer of tiles, has performed his task with painstaking skill. ABOVE: garden paths in the 17th-century palace built by Moulay Ismael in Tangier are of brick with accent tiles. OVERLEAF: traditional Islamic designs are not judged by the originality of their designs but by the combinations of colors. Innovative tiles in the Hassan II mosque in Casablanca point away from the ages-old traditional Islamic patterns.**

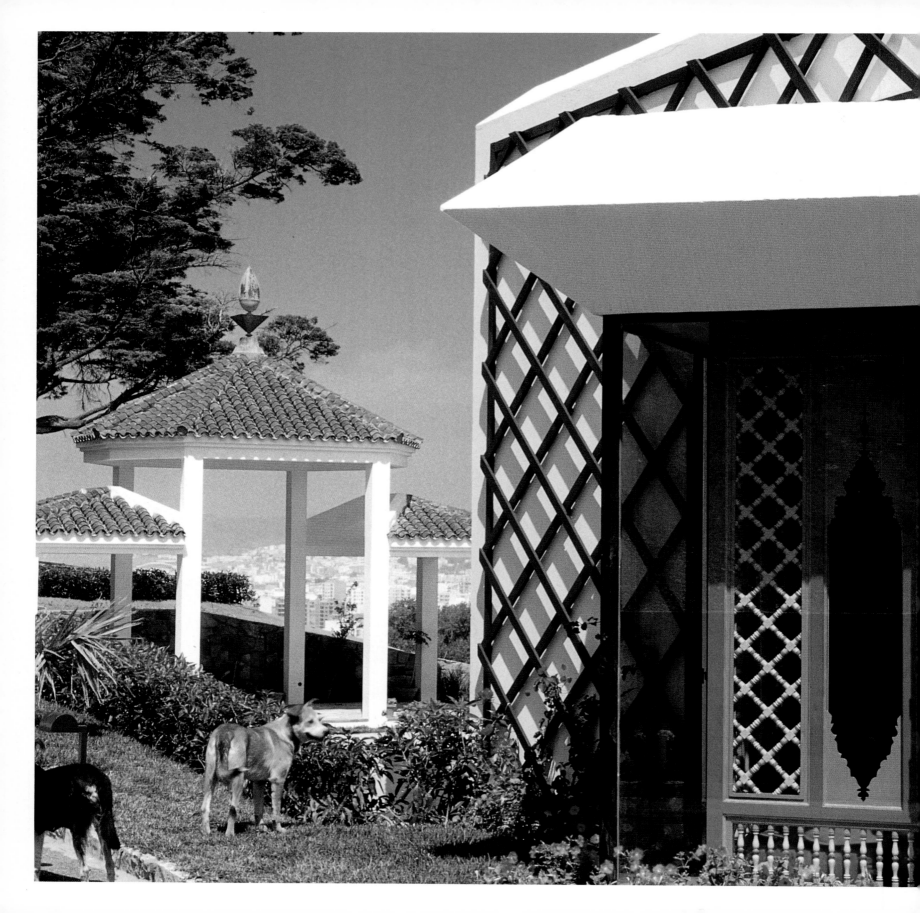

# A Contemporary Renovation

With deft window treatments, American designer Stewart Church turned a nondescript modern house near Tangier into a dramatic neo-Islamic weekend retreat for Mina and Salah Balafrej.

MOROCCANS AND FOREIGNERS ALIKE ARE REDISCOVERING TANGIER'S centuries-old international appeal. Ideally located for weekend excursions across the Mediterranean to nearby Spain, the city offers a unique Moroccan-European life-style. King Hassan has renovated a palace in Tangier. So too has a princess from the Middle East. ✋ Add to the list Mina and Salah Balafrej from Rabat. Expatriate American designer Stewart Church helped the couple reinterpret an existing modern house on Sharf Hill, overlooking the harbor. With Church's renovation, it has become one of Morocco's most dramatic contemporary private residences. Of special significance are the houses's windows, doors, and latticework. Here it is clear that contemporary homeowners are beginning to embellish their houses' exteriors. Knowing that Moroccans in the 19th century were fond of

193

bright colors, Church convinced the Balafrejs to look back in time and be equally bold. The house's formal Moroccan reception room with its striking red *tadelakt* walls is a tour de force of neo-Islamic design.

Other rooms contain Moroccan and European furniture arrangements—new and old—which combine to make the Balafrej house one of the most fresh and sophisticated mixes of traditional Moroccan and Western design in the country.

**LEFT: a large glass-top table for serving food at parties reflects the striking red *tadelakt* interior of the reception room. Handpainted doors were designed by Church and made in the souk. ABOVE: especially noteworthy is the latticework Church designed for the facades.**

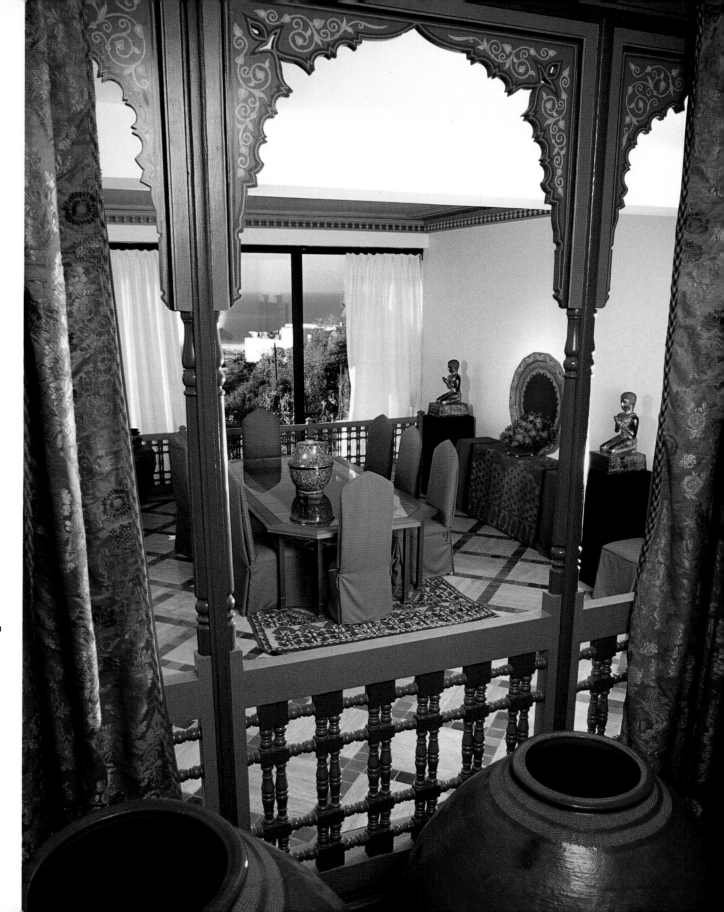

A mezzanine sitting room opens onto a dining room, with views of the Mediterranean.

ABOVE: Moorish-style architectural symmetry dramatizes the flow of space. FAR LEFT: a sitting room includes European sofas and Moroccan-inspired torchères, tables, and chairs designed by Church. LEFT: detail of painted dome in living room.

# A Bit of Old England

IN THE LATE 1940s, DAVID HERBERT, SON OF THE FIFTEENTH EARL of Pembroke, moved permanently from Wilton, his ancestral home in England, to Tangier. ✋ The doyen of the city's international foreign colony, he remembers the 1950s and 1960s, when Tangier was a mecca for hedonists anxious to experience the go-for-broke pleasures of North Africa; and he appreciates that times have changed. Tangier is now a quiet haven for cosmopolites grateful to live comfortably and privately—in Morocco yet within sight of Europe. ✋ Caroubia, Herbert's rambling two-story Provençal-style pink house—with shutters painted a startling Matisse turquoise—was the retreat of the 19th-century mystic Sidi Amar. It is set in La Montaigne, a popular residential area where the king and several foreign princes and princesses have palaces. ✋ One passes through arched Moroccan door-

OPPOSITE: the wall surrounding the heavy wooden front door is inset with sea shells; a 17th-century William Kent mirror and 19th-century French prints decorate the foyer. Out back, a pair of contemporary Italian ceramic guard dogs flanks a terrace leading to Herbert's vast, semitropical garden. A French wrought-iron chair in the shape of a swan lends a note of whimsy and charm to the garden. RIGHT: full of 18th- and 19th-century English, French, and Italian furniture and paintings, the European-style drawing rooms in Caroubia are entered through Moroccan-style doorways. Vases of fresh flowers compete for space on tables crowded with photographs of well-known friends—the Queen Mother, Barbara Hutton, and Cecil Beaton among them.

ways into what is otherwise a very European household. Like other Tangier houses owned by European expatriates who surrounded themselves with the familiar, Caroubia makes few concessions to its Moroccan location. Indeed, Herbert's cozy, chintz-filled rooms are full of mainly English furniture as well as paintings by Van Dyck, Reynolds, Augustus John, Cecil Beaton, Claudio Bravo, and Rex Whistler.

The 18th- and 19th-century English chairs, sofas, bureaus, picture and mirror frames are gilded, lacquered, and often carved. "Directoire, regency, rococo, and chinoiserie—I love them all. It's hard to choose," says Herbert. The surprise is the palette. Walls of egg-yolk yellow, lime green, and Rajastan pink all testify to Herbert's exuberant style. "White is so boring," he confides.

**The lime colored walls of the main salon are hung with paintings brought by Herbert from Wilton, his ancestral home. Van Dyck's "Countess of Pembroke" hangs over the fireplace between a pair of 18th-century Italian mirrors; across the room is a self-portrait by Sir Thomas Lawrence.**

# Color

A primary blue hand of Fatima stands in sharp relief against the hot pink of a truck's splash guard.

BENEATH MOROCCO'S CLOUDLESS BLUE SKIES ARE BONE-WHITE towns and multicolored fishing ports. The same landscape can be a tapestry of bright wildflowers in spring and a monotonous carpet of stubble in summer. Stalls in the souks spill over with multihued fruits and vegetables. Woven baskets mix colors that clash brilliantly. Tiles offer a kaleidoscope of color. ✋ Tradition-steeped artisans in Morocco continue to demonstrate an innate color sense as compelling today as it was to Matisse in the early 20th century. Palace throne rooms, Berber houses in the Atlas, bolts of cloth in Chaouen, sugar cones wrapped in paper, women's veils and caftans, men's leather slippers—there is color everywhere in Morocco. It is in tiles, in fabrics, and on walls, shutters, and doors. Subtle and soft, bold and bright, color is part of Morocco's magic.

205

OPPOSITE: a dappled veil shields the face of a woman in Taroudant. LEFT: a rich red banner incorporating the Moroccan star is draped across a palm-frond fence.

**LEFT:** the stark white that is such a signature of the walls and doorways of Chaouen is created by white lye. **OPPOSITE:** banners of many colors are hung beneath the reed roofs that cover the aisles of many souks.

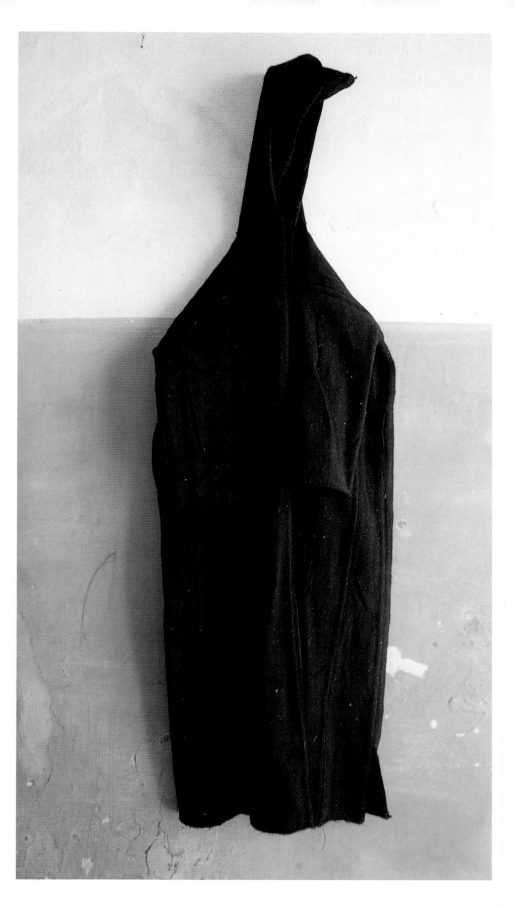

OPPOSITE: at a café in
Rabat, tables and chairs
are painted blue;
the color is believed to ward
off evil spirits. LEFT:
the walls of a courtyard in
Asilah are painted lime
and off-white; black is a
traditional color for
men's *burnooses.*

Modern calligraphic
tiles at the Hassan II mosque are
in a rich panoply of colors.

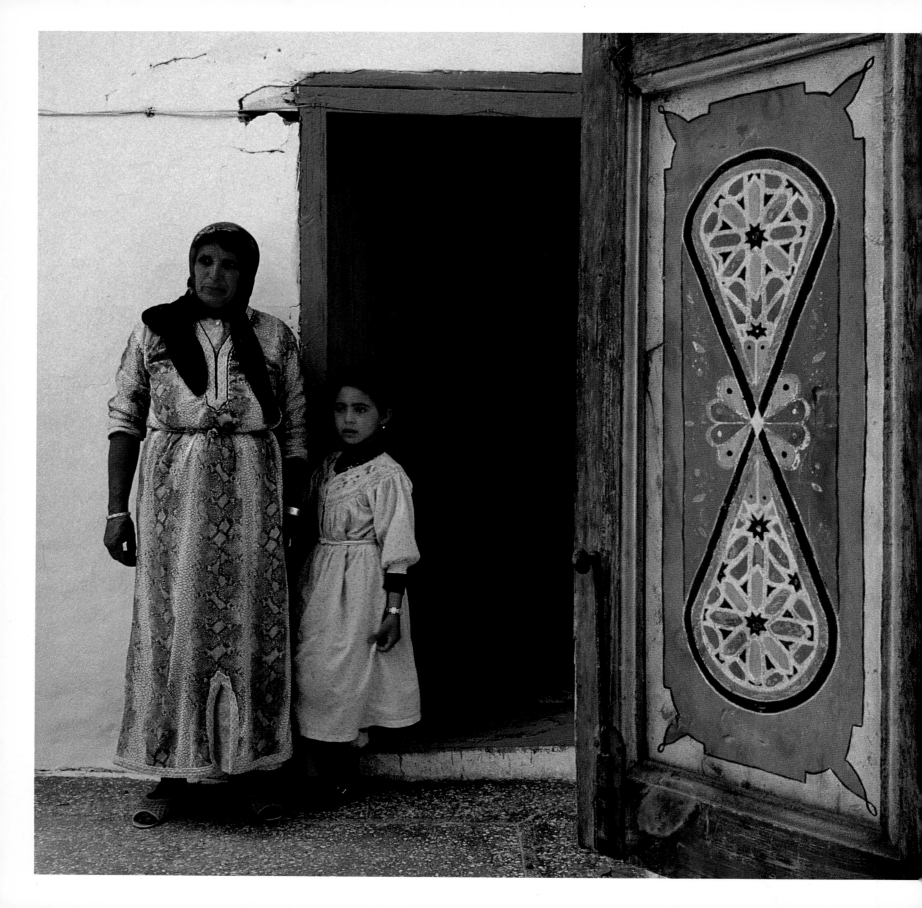

# A Caidal Farmhouse

A servant and her child wait for guests to arrive at a mid-19th-century farmhouse built by caid M'Barek M'Addi near Neknafi outside Essaouira. Doors and shutters were decorated by itinerant painters from Marrakesh.

FOR THREE GENERATIONS, THE MID-19TH-CENTURY FARMHOUSE built of stone and adobe has been in the same family. High on a hill within sight of the Atlantic Ocean, the enormous complex of courtyards, grain-storage rooms, stables, and living quarters is near the village of Neknafi. ✋ "It was built by my grandfather, caid M'Barek M'Addi," explains Moulay Rhounimi. "It took him four hours on horseback to ride here from his palace in Essaouira. He came to oversee his lands and meet with his tenant farmers. They brought all their problems to him to solve." ✋ Today, the caidal estate is still maintained by heirs who take turns coming for weekends from their homes in Essaouira and Marrakesh to maintain a way of life little different than that of their ancestors. ✋ They park their cars in cobblestoned courtyards where camels and donkeys unload grain for

215

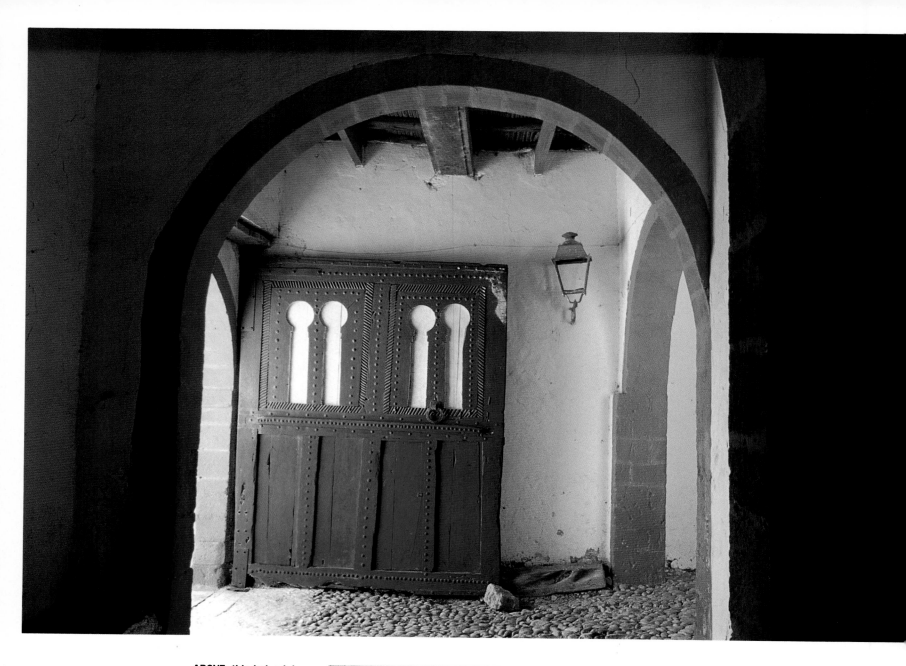

**ABOVE:** this *bab ed dar*, entrance door, leads from the whitewashed courtyard with its ochre trim to inside living quarters. Unlike European doors, most Moroccan doors are not mounted on hinges. They are mounted on pivots because of their great size. **RIGHT:** bags of grain await threshing in the courtyard.

thrashing. Surrounding white-washed buildings with bright blue doors have windows trimmed in yellow ocher, traditional colors of the sky and the earth. Servants, mainly young girls, rush to pour water from antique silver pitchers into basins where their dusty employers and guests may wash their hands. Quickly, they return to the fin de siècle kitchen, then bustle into the reception rooms laden with heavy trays of mint tea and fresh-baked pastries.

Hung with ancestor paintings, the rooms were decorated by painters from Marrakesh who came by horseback to festoon doors, ceilings, and shutters with abstract flower bouquets, now faded by rain, sun, and neglect. "The house has been this way for as long as I can remember," says Moulay Rhounimi. "We don't see any reason for modernizing."

**FROM TOP: a saddle is decorated with pieces of multicolored plastic. The courtyard is paved with rubble. A hole has been cut in this door as an entryway for the farmhouse's many cats.**

217

A hand-colored photograph of caid M'Barek M'Addi hangs in the farmhouse's main reception room. The cut velvet brocade is popular today; the hassocks are made of Moroccan leather.

ABOVE AND LEFT: a copy
of the Koran lies locked
inside this massive
handpainted chest, which dates
from the 19th century.

# A Berber-Style Farmhouse

FORERUNNERS OF THE CURRENT INTERNATIONAL BUILDING BOOM IN the Palmeraie outside Marrakesh, the Bernard Levys were pioneers. Residents of Casablanca and Paris, the Moroccan-born couple built a vacation "farmhouse" beneath the towering palm. A high adobe wall keeps the farmhouse from view, while a constant cacophony of braying donkeys, quacking ducks, crowing roosters, and gobbling turkeys helps to conceal the fact the house is only fifteen minutes from downtown. ✋ "We wanted the Marrakesh house to have an earthy, Berber quality," the couple says to explain the building's exterior. It is made from thin red bricks with beige mortar in between, a characteristic of villages in the southern Sahara. ✋ Nestled in a garden full of olive and citrus trees and surrounded by fields of wheat dappled with red poppies, the one-story house's outside windows are painted

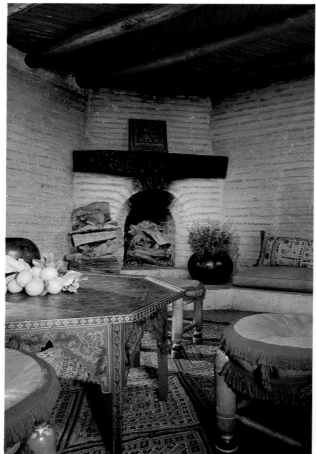

ABOVE: striped silk pillows
are stuffed into a Berber
chest that has been painted
inside and out. RIGHT:
in the dining room, wood and
leather stools surround
the hand-painted table.
OPPOSITE: embroidered
curtains from Fez are
used to conceal the sleeping
alcove. The spread is
a French lace tablecloth; the
pillows are from the souk.

bright blue. Antique Moroccan doors inside the house reemphasize the Levys' insistence on historic local authenticity.

With herringbone floors of terra-cotta, burnt umber, and olive-colored baby bricks, the living room has coffee tables made from native thuya wood from Essaouira. Off-white muslin is used both for curtains and to cover modern sofas.

The "Berber country" look continues in an adjacent guesthouse. Entered through dazzling blue doors, bedrooms full of antique handpainted furniture are off an all-white courtyard the floor of which is covered with bright yellow-and-blue tiles.

"The house is exactly what we wanted. It is barefoot, Moroccan country," the Levys are happy to say. "The way we live in Marrakesh is a happy change from Casablanca and Paris."

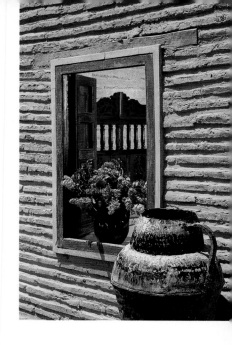

OPPOSITE: muslin curtains and upholstery lend an air of coolness to the living room, with its white tray ceiling. The furniture is handmade and contemporary. ABOVE: an iodized metal jug sits in the garden outside a bedroom window.

**ABOVE:** a hand-painted cupboard is used for storing pottery in the kitchen. **ABOVE RIGHT:** a painted wood panel adds a further decorative element to the kitchen. **RIGHT:** chickens have nested outside the kichen door. **FAR RIGHT:** mattresses air in the tiled courtyard outside of the guest house.

# A North African Paradise

Restored to their original North African lushness by designer Yves Saint Laurent and business partner Pierre Berge, this dreamlike garden surrounds the 1920s Marrakesh studio of french artist Jacques Majorelle.

RESTORED AND OPENED TO THE PUBLIC BY YVES SAINT LAURENT and his business partner Pierre Berge, the Majorelle Gardens in Marrakesh were laid out in the 1920s by French painter Jacques Majorelle, son of Louis Majorelle, the renowned Art Nouveau cabinetmaker. They are a walled-in oasis of dark green beauty, with buildings and walkways of *bleu de travail*, a high-key cobalt blue seen throughout France in workmen's overalls and introduced to Morocco by Majorelle. ✋ Yves Saint Laurent, who has frequently revealed his affection for Berber color combinations in his collections, strolls down pink concrete paths in the Majorelle Gardens past blue and green pergolas, lemon-yellow flowerpots, and apple-green doors, windows, and balustrades. ✋ Pruned, clipped, and watered by eight gardeners, hundreds of different species of native North African and

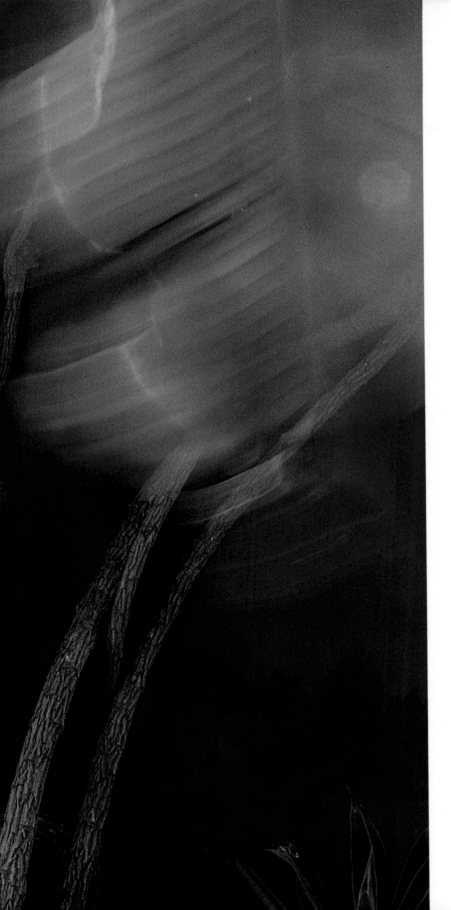

imported trees, vines, grasses, plants, and flowers combine to make the Majorelle Gardens a Rousseauesque sanctuary of cool shade in what can be a very hot, dusty city. A lover of *jardins exotiques*, the painter Matisse would have loved to stroll through the groves of towering bamboo and American coconut palms; beneath the trellises covered by multicolored bougainvillea; beside pools full of papyri, lotus flowers, and lily pads; along *allées* bordered with orange and yellow nasturtiums and hot-pink geraniums.

"I remember when Majorelle's widow gave her husband's paintings away. No one appreciated him. After his death, the gardens fell into ruin," says an old-time Marrakesh resident. "But today, his canvases are in demand and the gardens are always exquisitely maintained." Indeed, a visit to the ·Majorelle gardens is a major reason for many people to come to Morocco.

**A large banana leaf flutters in the wind in front of a gray and yellow door designed by Yves Saint Laurent.**

TOP: carp swim lazily back and forth in a tiled reflecting pool. ABOVE: vermilion and fuchsia bougainvillea cover trellises along pink-tinted concrete paths. RIGHT: red and pink geraniums, orange nasturtiums, and large yellow jars present a colorful, painterly exterior to the outside of a pavilion.

The richness of the garden's *bleu de travail,* or workers's blue, walls brings palms into sharp relief.

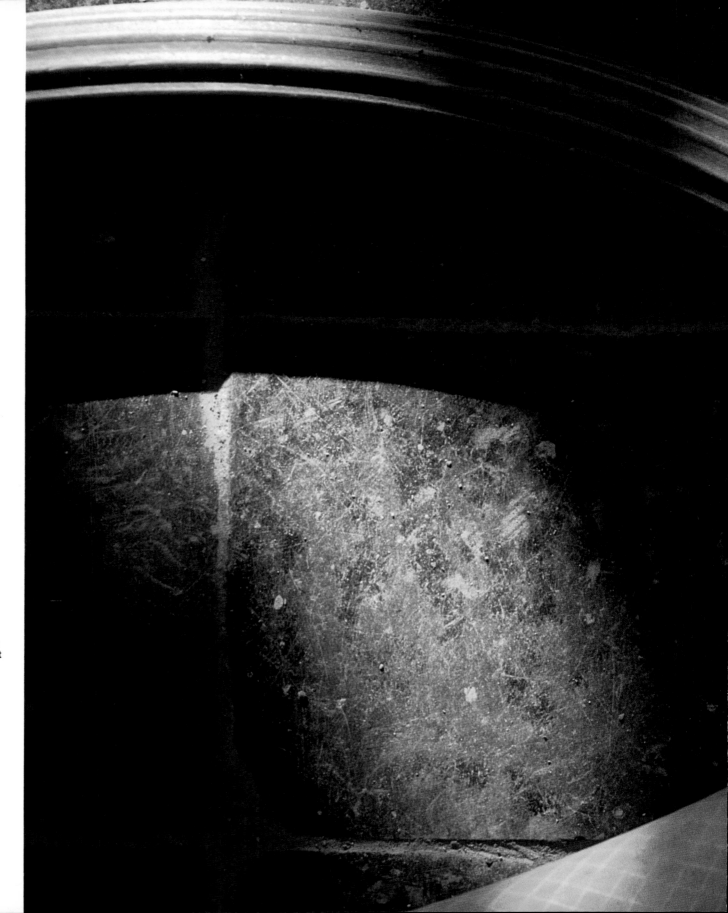

Crossed garden hoses
and fallen bougainvillea
petals create an abstract
design on the tiled
walk in the garden.

Majorelle created
a Rousseauesque sanctuary
of cool shade in what can
be a hot and dusty city.

# Travel to Morocco

FOR THOSE FLYING FROM THE United States to Morocco, Royal Air Maroc is the only airline that flies directly from New York City. Flights leave New York in the early evening and arrive in Casablanca the following morning.

There are direct connecting flights from Casablanca for Tangier, Agadir, and Marrakesh.

Flights from Morocco to the United States depart the airport in Casablanca in the morning, arriving in New York in the afternoon the same day.

There are daily flights to and from all major European cities on Royal Air Maroc and other European carriers.

All major automobile rental agencies have offices at the Casablanca airport. Car rentals are expensive; therefore, a group traveling together to Morocco may wish to consider renting a car, or a van, with a driver. It may turn out to be less expensive.

The average length of stay in Morocco is seven to fifteen days. In that time, a great deal can be seen. Distances between interesting towns and cities are not large, and traveling them rarely takes more than a half day or a full day. The roads are good. And the scenery and stopoff points are beautiful and interesting.

Ramadan, a religious festival that vaguely parallels the Christian Lent, occurs in the spring. It is observed by all faithful Moroccans, who may neither drink nor eat from dawn until dusk. During Ramadan many restaurants and shops are closed during the day. However, they are open at night, and hotel restaurants remain open for guests and tourists.

French is spoken throughout Morocco, together with Arabic and Berber. English is spoken by hotel and restaurant staffs almost everywhere.

In Morocco, unlike other Moslem countries, outsiders are not permitted to enter mosques.

Female visitors to Morocco will feel more comfortable in blouses, skirts, and pants—rather than shorts—when exploring the cities and towns.

# Shoppers' Guide

THE FOLLOWING IS IN NO WAY A list of "recommended" shops and craftsmen, but it is a place to get started both in Morocco and Great Britain. Moroccan cities are full of stores selling Moroccan crafts, and its souks are full of talented craftsmen. One must go, see, decide for oneself. In the last few years, a number of shops and stores in Britain have developed their ethnic arts and crafts ranges, and a few focus exclusively on Morocco. There is no question, it is easier to deal with a "home base" outlet than it is to search out, bargain over, and go through the hassle of shipping something from Morocco. But shopping in Morocco is great fun, although you must keep the rules of the game very much in mind.

It is often difficult for the novice to tell the difference between yesterday's treasure and today's reproduction, especially when the seller insists that everything over fifty years old is "antique." The system demands comparative shopping before bargaining down the price for *anything and everything* for a good deal less than originally asked. Because bargaining is expected in Morocco, store owners expect to settle on a price anywhere from 25 to 50 percent less than originally asked, both in and out of the souks.

When shopping in Morocco, one must be alert to the fact that if a guide takes you to a store, or your hotel recommends a store, the chances are good that the prices you'll be quoted will be as much as 50 percent over what the store owner would have started bargaining at if you'd gone there alone. Because "those who help" will get a cut of the deal, to shop on your own is to save a great deal of money.

# Morocco

**CASABLANCA**

**Art de Fez**
**Rue General Laperine, No. 6**
**Tel: 31.00.30**

**FEZ**

**Au Petit Bazar de Bon Accueil**
**35 Talaa Sghira**
**Medina Ancienne**
**Tel: 337.64**

**Boutique Majid**
**Abdelmajid Rais El Fenni**
**66 Rue des Chretiens**
**Tel: 388.92**

**MARRAKESH**

**Adolfo de Valasco**
**Hotel La Mamounia**
**Tel: 32.38, 32.82**

**Bazar du Sud**
**117 Souk des Tapis**
**Tel: 430.04**

**Chez Alaoui**
**Souk Shouari**
**Ghassoul No. 42**

**Chez Les Brodeuses Arab**
**12 Rue Rahba Lakdima**
**Tel: 448.55**

Coopartim
Ensemble Artisinal
Avenue Mohammed V
Tel: 436.64

Fandak El Fatmi
Bab Ftouh

Fandak El Quarzazi
Bab Ftouh

La Lampe d'Aladin
99 and 70 bis Rue Semmarine
Tel: 434.84

Mamounia Arts
47 Rue Dar El Bacha
Bab Doukkala

Moroccan Arts
67 Sabeb Mouley Hadj
El Kssour

L'Oiseau Bleu
3 Rue Tarik Ibn Ziad

L'Orientaliste
15 Rue de la Liberte
Tel: 340.74, 304.43

Reminiscence
Sourya No. 7
Tel: 315.18

RABAT

Gallerie Cheremetieff
16 bis Rue Aannaba

SAFI

Serghini Ahmed
7 Souk des Poteries
Tel: 23.41

TANGIER

Adolfo de Velasco
28 Blvd. Mohammed V
Tel: 388-58

Arditti
87 Rue de la Liberte

Bazar Sebou
18 Rue Sebou

Boutique Majid
66 Rue des Chretiens

# Great Britain

Chandni Chowk
1 Harlequins
Paul Street
Exeter
Devon
EX4 3TT
Tel: 01392 410201
(Rugs, pottery)

Graham & Green
4 Elgin Crescent
London W11
Tel: 0171 727 4594
(Lamps, pottery, wooden articles)

Joss Graham Oriental Textiles
10 Eccleston Street
London SW1 9LT
Tel: 0171 730 4370
(Pottery and textiles)

The Kilim & Nomadic Rug Gallery
5 Shepherds Walk
London NW3 5UL
Tel: 0171 435 8972
(Rugs)

The Kilim House
28A Pickets Street,
London SW12 8QB
Tel: 0181 675 3122

Liberty plc
210/220 Regent Street
London W1R 6AH
Tel: 0171 734 1234
(Pottery, mirrors, fabric)

Moroccan Rugs and Weavings
5A Calabria Road
London N5 1JB
Tel: 0171 226 7908
(Rugs)

Nice Irma's
46 Goodge Street
London W1P 1FJ
Tel: 0171 580 6921
(Pottery, jewelry, mirrors)

On Show
19 Short's Gardens
Covent Garden
London WC2H 9AT
Tel: 0171 240 9731
(Pottery)

Verandah
15B Blenheim Crescent
London W11 2EE
Tel: 0171 792 9289
(Pottery and lanterns)

# Antiques

OLD POTTERY; EMBROIDERY; FUR-niture; jewelry; rugs; handcarved and painted wood doors, windows, and chests; wrought-iron grillwork to cover windows: they can all be found in every Moroccan city and town, in souks, in shops, at street markets. Moroccans and visitors alike join ranks to discover and bargain over the country's occasionally old, and very often made-to-look-old arts and crafts. When buying anything "antique" at what can be a high price, *caveat emptor* must be kept uppermost in mind.

# Pottery

POTTERY IS MADE TODAY throughout Morocco. Clay kitchen pots, often earth-toned and glazed, are sold outside major towns along the roads. Colorful handmade ceramics are made pri-marily in Fez and Safi, where centuries-old kilns are still fired up daily. Ready-made ceramics abound, but it is also possible to request special orders for shipping abroad. The majority of Moroccan ceramic styles and colors continue to be the same as those in the 17th and 18th centuries.

## FEZ

Fekhari Hamida
Quartier Industriel
Route de Tissa
Tel: 493.22, 496.88

# Wood

THUYA WOOD IS SIMILAR TO burled walnut in appearance. Varying in shades from dark mahogany to sprightly pear or cherry, thuya grows in the forests around Essaouira. Thousands of woodcarvers sit daily making boxes, chess sets, frames, obe-lisks, and bookends, most of which are exported to Europe, where prices are often 500 percent higher than in Essaouira.

## CASABLANCA

Az-El-Arab Benlamlih
24 Bis Rue de Briey
Bd. Mustapha El Maani

Centre de Formation Professionnelle
327 Blvd. 2 Mars
Tel: 817.09

Chraibi Mohamed
6 Rue General Laparine
Tel: 31.00.30

Slimani Mohamed
Lot. Laayoune No. 31
Ain Borja
(near Super Lait)

## ESSAOUIRA

Bazar du Sud Marocain
16 Rue Abdelaziz El Fechtal
Tel: 47.26.21

Frederic Damgaard
1 Rue Hajjeli
Tel: 47.35.06

## QUEZZANE

Cooperative Artisanale de
Tisserands Quezzane
Ensemble Artisanale
Tel: 74.62

# Custom Craftsmen

LOCALS INEVITABLY HAVE THEIR bedspreads, curtains, furniture, lamps, tiles, doors, and the like crafted by specialized workers in the souk. Unsurpassed craftsmanship is readily available at prices that make Morocco one of the world's least expensive sources for home furnishings. Among the most skillful are the following.

## CASABLANCA

**Ste. Somatraf**
**195 Ave. Hassan II**
**Tel: 26.38.78 / 26.72.98**
**(Plasterwork columns, tables, etc.)**

## FEZ

**Abdou Alaoui**
**Galerie Helio**
**15 Rue Karia**
**Tel: 203.45**
**(Lamps, lanterns, chandeliers, torcheres)**

**Comatrac**
**69 Blvd. Mohamed V**
**Tel: 232.05, 246.76**
**(Contemporary wool and cotton fabrics suitable for furniture, curtains, bedspreads, etc.)**

**Fekhari Mohamed**
**Quartier Industriel**
**Route de Tissa**
**Tel: 493.22**
**(Ceramics)**

**Intexa**
**150 Blvd. Mohamed V**
**Tel: 225.32, 225.33**
**(Contemporary wool and cotton fabrics suitable for furniture, curtains, bedspreads, etc.)**

**Magasin Artisanal**
**Sabat Lahyadrine, No. 3 V.A.**
**Tel: 333.83**
**(Local handicrafts)**

## MARRAKESH

**Boujmiai Ahmed**
**Souk Essarajine No. 116**
**Tel: 413.83, 418.17**
**(Etched glass)**

**Kharbibi Moulay Ahmen**
**Fandak El Amrie Sidi Abdelle**
**Azize Dar El Bacha No. 10**
**(Wood carvings)**

## MIDELT

**Soeurs Franciscaines**
**Kasbah Myriem**
**Tel: 058.24.43**
**(Handmade rugs, linens, bedspreads, etc.)**

## RABAT

**Art Des Oudayas Sur Bois**
**150 Place des Oudayas**
**Tel: 268.09**
**(Wood carvings)**

# Glossary

**agdal**—garden

**ajjan**—mixer of plaster of Paris

**bab**—monumental gate

**bab ed dar**—entrance or door

**babouches**—man's slippers

**bejmats**—half-bricks enameled on one side and used as floor covering

**burnoose**—man's hooded cloak, often worn over a *djellaba*

**caid**—Moslem ruler of a province

**chems**—small openings in a window, usually made from plaster of Paris with openwork or stained glass

**courzya**—striped apron worn by Rif mountain women

**dar**—house, abode, domain

**djellaba**—man's robe

**fakhkhar**—ceramist

**fantasia**—Berber horseman's display

**farrash** (pl. *farrasha*)—tile setter who puts *zelliges* directly into a wall

**flij**—woven strips for tents

**gebs** (or *jibs*)—plaster of Paris, gypsum, or stucco

**ghabbar** (pl. *ghabbara*)—artist who joins *zelliges* together, usually with cement and plaster of Paris

**haik**—woman's dress

**hammam**—steam bath

**hanbel**—roughly woven, plain-weave striped blankets and wall hangings made by Berbers

**jamur**—roof spike made of enameled baked clay or metal with up to five balls of diminishing size and often capped with the national emblem, a star inside a crescent moon

**kasbah**—desert domain of a single family and dependents

**koubbas**—tombs of *marabout*, local saints

**ksar** (pl. *ksour*)—desert tribal fortress sheltering a village community

**maallem**—master crafter

**marabout**—local saint

**medersa**—Moslem institute of higher learning connected to a mosque

**medina**—the "old town"

**mellah**—Jewish quarter of a medina

**moucharaby**—panel of wooden openwork used in balustrades and furniture, also to cover harem windows

**pisé**—rammed earth

**qermud**—roof tile

**qubba**—cupola or dome, often in a main room

**rahalia**—large decorative plates made in Fez

**riyad**—inside garden or courtyard

**souk**—central market, a collection of stalls

**sultan**—Moslem ruler of the country

**tadelakt**—Moroccan wall and occasionally floor treatment comparable to Italian stucco, made of sand and quicklime and polished by stone

**taksir**—cutter of *zelliges*

**tizi**—mountain pass

**vizier**—Moslem minister of state

**wust ed dar**—patio

**zawwaq** (pl. *zawwaqa*)—craftsman who paints on wood

**zelliges**—mosaic tiles of enameled terra-cotta

**zwaq**—painting on wood

# Bibliography

Barbour, Neville. *Morocco*. London: Thames & Hudson, 1965.

*Blue Guide to Morocco*. New York: W. W. Norton, 1988.

Bowles, Paul. *Points in Time*. London: Peter Owen, 1982.

———. *The Sheltering Sky*. London: John Lehmann, 1949.

———. *Let It Come Down*. London: John Lehmann, 1952.

———. *The Spider's House*. New York City: Random House, 1955.

Bryans, Robin. *Morocco, Land of the Farthest West*. London: Faber & Faber, 1965.

Canetti, Elias. *The Voices of Marrakesh*. London: Marion Boyars, 1967.

Carrier, Robert. *A Taste of Morocco*. New York: Clarkson N. Potter, Inc., 1987.

D'Ucel, Jeanne. *Berber Art*. Norman, Okla.: University of Oklahoma Press, 1932.

Ellingham, Mark, and McVeigh, Shaun. *The Rough Guide to Morocco*. London: Harrap-Columbus, 1988.

Flint, Bert. *Tapis et Tissage*. Vol. 2 of *Formes et Symboles dans les Arts Maghrebis*. Tangier: Imprimie E.M.I., 1974.

*Fodor's North Africa*. New York: Fodor's Travel Publications, Inc., 1988.

Gellner, Ernest. *Saints of the Atlas*. London: Weidenfeld & Nicolson, 1969.

Harris, Walter. *Morocco That Was*. London: Eland Books, 1921.

Hoag, John Douglas. *Western Islamic Architecture*. New York: Braziller, 1963.

Holiday, Jane. *Blue Guide/Morocco*. New York: W. W. Norton, 1989.

Kay, Shirley. *Morocco*. London: Naamara Publications Ltd., 1980.

Landau, Rom. *The Beauty of Morocco*. London: Evans Brothers Ltd., 1951.

———. *The Kasbas of Southern Morocco*. London: Faber Press, 1979.

Maxwell, Gavin. *Lords of the Atlas*. London: Longmans, Green and Co. Ltd., 1966.

Montagne, Robert. *The Berbers*. London: Frank Cass & Co. Ltd., 1973.

Paccard, Andre. *Traditional Islamic Craft in Moroccan Architecture*. Saint-Jorioz, France: Editions Atelier 74, 1980.

Phelan, Nancy. *Morocco Is a Lion*. Melbourne: Quartet Books Australia Pty Ltd., 1982.

Rice, David Talbot. *Islamic Art*. London: Thames & Hudson, New York: Oxford University Press, 1975.

Rogerson, Barnaby. *Cadogan Guides: Morocco*. Chester, Conn.: The Globe Pequot Press, 1989.

Sijelmass, M. *Les Arts Traditionnels au Maroc*. Courbevoie (Paris): ACR Edition/Vilo., 1986.

Textile Museum, Washington, D.C.: *From the Far West: Carpets and Textiles of Morocco*, 1980.

# Acknowledgments

ONE OF THE GREAT PLEASURES IN producing *Morocco* was to meet and work with so many people on both sides of the Atlantic who share our love of this great kingdom. The help, support, and enthusiasm shown to us by the Moroccan National Tourist Office and Moroccan diplomats and government officials, as well as homeowners, hoteliers, designers, and friends living in Morocco, allowed the work on this book to proceed smoothly from its conception.

The prospect of traveling to and from Morocco half a dozen times over the last two years with over three hundred pounds of photography equipment appeared ominous. Mustapha Benkirane, New York general manager of Royal Air Maroc, smoothed the way. Once we had landed, Ambassador Abdeslam Jaidi made sure land arrangements were equally well arranged. Our palace driver, Mohammed Alif, was in constant amazement at the hours we put in, the rough roads we wanted to drive down, the distances we insisted upon covering, and the people, places, and things we photographed. To these gentlemen and all the anonymous people who were always there to help, we say, "Thank you. Without your help, we could not have accomplished so much."

To all the many homeowners who were kind enough to allow us to photograph their properties, we are especially grateful. From Tangier to Taroudant, from Casablanca to Marrakesh, doors to villas, palaces, and apartments were graciously opened to allow us to photograph examples of Moroccan interior design and architecture, much of which had never been recorded before.

It is with tremendous gratitude and with great hope that they will enjoy the fruits of our mutual labors in producing the book that we wish to thank: Issam Lamdouar, director, and Sand Seghrouchni of the Moroccan National Tourist Office, New York City; Ambassador Driss Slaoui; Michel Benisty, Interrent, Casablanca; Jacques Bouriot, director, Mohammed Hammouti, assistant director, and Liliane Boucetta, secretary, as well as the concierge staff, of the Hotel La Mamounia, Marrakesh; Alami Myjat, director general, Hotel Palais Jamai, Fez; Guy Crawford, director general, Hotel Mansour, Casablanca; Bruno Hill, general manager, Hotel Gazelle d'Or, Taroudant;

Jean Paul Lance, former manager of the Hotel Tishka, Marrakesh; Robert Swartzberg, general director, Hotel Minza, Tangier; Louis Bernard, public relations director, Bouygues, Paris.

Very special recognition goes to Bob Ciano, art director, *Travel & Leisure,* and Paige Rense, editor-in-chief, and Tom Sullivan, art director, *Architectural Digest,* who gave us Moroccan assignments. Continued gratitude to photography assistants Andrew Warren, Majid Yadini, and Marc Poujol; photo stylist Claire Lloyd; Dina Davidson, vice president, Duggal Photographic Color Lab, New York City; Connie Uzzo, public relations director, Yves Saint Laurent, Inc., New York City; Christopher Forbes, vice chairman, *Forbes* magazine; Robert Jerofi; Jacqueline Foissac; Bill Willis; T. R. Lawrence and Linda O'Leary, Nomads, Santa Fe, New Mexico; James F. Jereb, The Souk, Santa Fe; Abdou Alaoui; and Missouri Abdelaouhab.

Of special significance was the initial support of the book given by Gael Towey, creative director, *Martha Stewart Living,* when she was at Clarkson Potter. Our gratitude also goes to Roy Finamore. He continued the project and provided skillful picture selection and deft text editing.

Finally, photographers will be interested to know that almost all photographs in the book were shot on Fujichrome Professional 100 film. Bruce Mitchell and Steve Hershel at Fuji headquarters in Carlstadt, New Jersey, and the staff at Polaroid in Cambridge, Massachusetts, were all extraordinarily supportive.

# Index